Jack C. Richards & Chuck Sandy

Passages

Third Edition

T0372636

1 B

Student's Book

CAMBRIDGE
UNIVERSITY PRESS

CAMBRIDGE
UNIVERSITY PRESS

University Printing House, Cambridge CB2 8BS, United Kingdom

One Liberty Plaza, 20th Floor, New York, NY 10006, USA

477 Williamstown Road, Port Melbourne, VIC 3207, Australia

314–321, 3rd Floor, Plot 3, Splendor Forum, Jasola District Centre, New Delhi – 110025, India

103 Penang Road, #05-06/07, Visioncrest Commercial, Singapore 238467

Cambridge University Press is part of the University of Cambridge.

It furthers the University's mission by disseminating knowledge in the pursuit of education, learning and research at the highest international levels of excellence.

www.cambridge.org
Information on this title: www.cambridge.org/9781107627727

First published 1998
Second edition 2008

20 19 18 17 16 15 14 13 12 11 10 9 8 7

Printed in Great Britain by CPI Group (UK) Ltd, Croydon CR0 4YY

A catalog record for this publication is available from the British Library.

ISBN 978-1-107-62705-5 Student's Book 1
ISBN 978-1-107-62701-7 Student's Book 1A
ISBN 978-1-107-62706-2 Student's Book 1B
ISBN 978-1-107-62725-3 Workbook 1
ISBN 978-1-107-62718-5 Workbook 1A
ISBN 978-1-107-62720-8 Workbook 1B
ISBN 978-1-107-62768-0 Teacher's Edition 1 with Assessment Audio CD/CD-ROM
ISBN 978-1-107-62754-3 Class Audio 1 CDs
ISBN 978-1-107-62769-7 Full Contact 1
ISBN 978-1-107-62771-0 Full Contact 1A
ISBN 978-1-107-62772-7 Full Contact 1B
ISBN 978-1-107-62762-8 DVD 1
ISBN 978-1-107-66626-9 Presentation Plus 1

Additional resources for this publication at www.cambridge.org/passages

Art direction, book design, layout services, and photo research: Q2A / Bill Smith
Audio production: John Marshall Media
Video production: Steadman Productions

Authors' Acknowledgments

A great number of people contributed to the development of *Passages Third Edition*. Particular thanks are owed to the following reviewers and institutions, as their insights and suggestions have helped define the content and format of the third edition:

Paulo A. Machado, Rio de Janeiro, Brazil; Simone C. Wanguestel, Niterói, Brazil; Athiná Arcadinos Leite, **ACBEU**, Salvador, Brazil; Lauren Osowski, **Adult Learning Center**, Nashua, NH, USA; Brenda Victoria, **AIF System**, Santiago, Dominican Republic; Alicia Mitchell-Boncquet, **ALPS Language School**, Seattle, WA, USA; Scott C. Welsh, **Arizona State University**, Tempe, AZ, USA; Silvia Corrêa, **Associação Alumni**, São Paulo, Brazil; Henrick Oprea, **Atlantic Idiomas**, Brasília, Brazil; Márcia Lima, **B.A. English School**, Goiânia, Brazil; Carlos Andrés Mejía Gómez, **BNC Centro Colombo Americano Pereira**, Pereira, Colombia; Tanja Jakimoska, **Brava Training**, Rio de Janeiro, Brazil; Paulo Henrique Gomes de Abreu, **Britannia International English**, Rio de Janeiro, Brazil; Gema Kuri Rodríguez, **Business & English**, Puebla, Mexico; Isabela Villas Boas, **Casa Thomas Jefferson**, Brasília, Brazil; Inara Lúcia Castillo Couto, **CEL-LEP**, São Paulo, Brazil; Ana Cristina Hebling Meira, **Centro Cultural Brasil-Estados Unidos**, Campinas, Brazil; Juliana Costa da Silva, **Centro de Cultura Anglo Americana**, Rio de Janeiro, Brazil; Heriberto Díaz Vázquez, **Centro de Investigación y Docencia Económicas**, Mexico City, Mexico; D. L. Dorantes-Salas, **Centro de Investigaciones Biológicas del Noroeste**, La Paz, Mexico; Elizabeth Carolina Llatas Castillo, **Centro Peruano Americano El Cultural**, Trujillo-La Libertad, Peru; Márcia M. A. de Brito, **Chance Language Center**, Rio de Janeiro, Brazil; Rosalinda Heredia, **Colegio Motolinia**, San Juan del Río, Mexico; Maria Regina Pereira Filgueirás, **College Language Center**, Londrina, Brazil; Lino Mendoza Rodriguez, **Compummunicate**, Izúcar de Matamoros, Mexico; Maria Lucia Sciamarelli, **Cultura Inglesa**, Campinas, Brazil; Elisabete Thess, **Cultura Inglesa**, Petrópolis, Brazil; Catarina M. B. Pontes Kruppa, **Cultura Inglesa**, São Paulo, Brazil; Sheila Lima, **Curso Oxford**, Rio de Janeiro, Brazil; Elaine Florencio, Beth Vasconcelos, **English House Corporate**, Rio de Janeiro, Brazil; Vasti Rodrigues e Silva, **Fox Idiomas**, Rio de Janeiro, Brazil; Ricardo Ramos Miguel Cézar, Walter Júnior Ribeiro Silva, **Friends Language Center**, Itapaci, Brazil; Márcia Maria Pedrosa Sá Freire de Souza, **IBEU**, Rio de Janeiro, Brazil; Jerusa Rafael, **IBEUV**, Vitória, Brazil; Lilianne de Souza Oliveira, **ICBEU**, Manaus, Brazil; Liviane Santana Paulino de Carvalho, **ICBEU**, São Luís, Brazil; Manuel Marrufo Vásquez, **iempac Instituto de Enseñanza del Idioma Ingles**, Tequila, Mexico; Nora Aquino, **Instituto de Ciencias y Humanidades Tabasco**, Villahermosa, Mexico; Andrea Grimaldo, **Instituto Laurens**, Monterrey, Mexico; Cenk Aykut, Staci Jenkins, Kristen Okada, **Interactive College of Technology**, Chamblee, GA, USA; Imeen Manahan-Vasquez, Zuania Serrano, **Interactive Learning Systems**, Pasadena, TX, USA; Nicholas J. Jackson, **Jackson English School**, Uruapan, Mexico; Marc L. Cummings, **Jefferson Community and Technical College**, Louisville, KY, USA; Solange Nery Veloso, **Nery e Filho Idiomas**, Rio de Janeiro, Brazil; Tomas Sparano Martins, **Phil Young's English School**, Curitiba, Brazil; Paulo Cezar Lira Torres, **PRIME Language Center**, Vitória, Brazil; Angie Vasconcellos, **Robin English School**, Petrópolis, Brazil; Barbara Raifsnider, **San Diego Community College District**, San Diego, CA, USA; James Drury de Matos Fonseca, **SENAC**, Fortaleza, Brazil; Manoel Fialho da Silva Neto, **SENAC**, Recife, Brazil; Marilyn Ponder, **Tecnológico de Monterrey**, Irapuato, Mexico; Linda M. Holden, **The College of Lake County**, Grayslake, IL, USA; Janaína da Silva Cardoso, **UERJ**, Rio de Janeiro, Brazil; Gustavo Reges Ferreira, Sandlei Moraes de Oliveira, **UFES**, Vitória, Brazil; Nancy Alarcón Mendoza, **UNAM, Facultad de Estudios Superiores Zaragoza**, Mexico City, Mexico; Rosa Awilda López Fernández, **UNAPEC**, Santo Domingo, Dominican Republic; Vera Lúcia Ratide, **Unilínguas**, São Leopoldo, Brazil; Elsa Yolanda Cruz Maldonado, **Universidad Autónoma de Chiapas**, Tapachula, Mexico; Deida Perea, **Universidad Autónoma de Ciudad Juárez**, Ciudad Juárez, Mexico; Gabriela Ladrón de Guevara de León, **Universidad Autónoma de la Ciudad de México**, Mexico City, Mexico; Juan Manuel Ardila Prada, **Universidad Autónoma de Occidente**, Cali, Colombia; Lizzete G. Acosta Cruz, **Universidad Autónoma de Zacatecas**, Fresnillo, Mexico; Ary Guel, Fausto Noriega, Areli Martínez Suaste, **Universidad Autónoma de Zacatecas**, Zacatecas, Mexico; Gabriela Cortés Sánchez, **Universidad Autónoma Metropolitana Azcapotzalco**, Mexico City, Mexico; Secundino Isabeles Flores, Guillermo Guadalupe Duran Garcia, Maria Magdalena Cass Zubiria, **Universidad de Colima**, Colima, Mexico; Alejandro Rodríguez Sánchez, **Universidad del Golfo de México Norte**, Orizaba, Mexico; Fabiola Meneses Argüello, **Universidad La Salle Cancún**, Cancún, Mexico; Claudia Isabel Fierro Castillo, **Universidad Politécnica de Chiapas**, Tuxtla Gutierrez, Mexico; Eduardo Aguirre Rodríguez, M.A. Carolina Labastida Villa, **Universidad Politécnica de Quintana Roo**, Cancún, Mexico; Gabriela de Jesús Aubry González, **Universidad TecMilenio Campus Veracruz**, Boca del Rio, Mexico; Frank Ramírez Marín, **Universidad Veracruzana**, Boca del Río, Mexico.

Additional thanks are owed to Alex Tilbury for revising the Self-assessment charts, Paul MacIntyre for revising the Grammar Plus section, and Karen Kawaguchi for writing the Vocabulary Plus section.

Welcome to Passages!

Congratulations! You have learned the basics; now it's time to raise your English to a whole new level.

Your journey through each unit of *Passages Third Edition* will include a range of activities that will **progressively expand your language ability** in a variety of contexts, including formal and informal communication.

Along the way, you will encounter frequent communication reviews and progress checks that will **systematically consolidate your learning**, while **additional grammar and vocabulary practice** is available whenever you need it in the Grammar Plus and Vocabulary Plus sections in the back of this book.

RAISING YOUR ENGLISH TO A WHOLE NEW LEVEL
Unique features to boost your English proficiency!

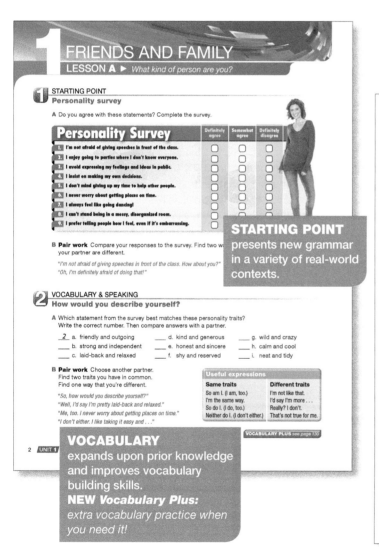

STARTING POINT presents new grammar in a variety of real-world contexts.

VOCABULARY expands upon prior knowledge and improves vocabulary building skills.
NEW *Vocabulary Plus:* *extra vocabulary practice when you need it!*

GRAMMAR is explored in context and builds on previously encountered structures.
Grammar Plus: *extra grammar explanations and practice when you need it!*

SPEAKING activities spark lively discussions focusing on interesting and relevant situations.

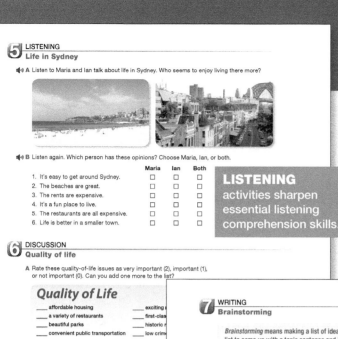

5 LISTENING
Life in Sydney

🔊 **A** Listen to Maria and Ian talk about life in Sydney. Who seems to enjoy living there more?

🔊 **B** Listen again. Which person has these opinions? Choose Maria, Ian, or both.

	Maria	Ian	Both
1. It's easy to get around Sydney.	☐	☐	☐
2. The beaches are great.	☐	☐	☐
3. The rents are expensive.	☐	☐	☐
4. It's a fun place to live.	☐	☐	☐
5. The restaurants are all expensive.	☐	☐	☐
6. Life is better in a smaller town.	☐	☐	☐

> **LISTENING** activities sharpen essential listening comprehension skills.

6 DISCUSSION
Quality of life

A Rate these quality-of-life issues as very important (2), important (1), or not important (0). Can you add one more to the list?

Quality of Life

___ affordable housing   ___ exciting
___ a variety of restaurants   ___ first-clas
___ beautiful parks   ___ historic
___ convenient public transportation   ___ low crim

B Pair work Which three issues are the most import considering where to live? Explain why.

*"I guess affordable housing and exciting nightlife are the m
find a place I could afford that was near someplace fun."*

*"I know what you mean. But for me, I guess low crime rate
I want to live somewhere where I feel safe. I don't mind if*

C Class activity Share your answers with your clas
mentioned most often?

24   UNIT 3   Exploring new cities

Passages Third Edition is a two-level course that will open the door to communicating with greater fluency and proficiency, with:

- **more sophisticated** real-world grammar and vocabulary,
- **thought-provoking** discussions and academic writing activities,
- **more challenging** listening and reading comprehension topics.

7 WRITING
Brainstorming

Brainstorming means making a list of ideas about a topic. Then you can use this list to come up with a topic sentence and ideas to support it.

A Group work Brainstorm as many ideas as you can to add to the dos and don'ts for living on a budget.

Living on a Tight Bu

Do	Don't
• compare prices	• buy the f
• look for sales	• buy bran
• check ads for used items	• use credi

B Group work Brainstorm dos and don'ts for one of

- getting over a bad cold
- staying safe in a bi

C Read this paragraph about living on a tight budget. T sentence and a similar paragraph about your topic u

[🗎 📁 🖼 🖨   A [_____]   B *I* U]

Living on a tight budget is easy if you follow som shopping. First of all, you should never buy somethi need to check at least a few other stores and go onl don't be in a hurry! If you take your time, you might now, ask a salesperson if there's going to be one so secondhand, items. You can check in the newspaper for. Finally, you might get a better price at some sto credit card, so be sure to ask about cash discounts.

D Pair work Exchange brainstorming lists and paragr Then answer the questions.

1. How many brainstorming ideas did your partner u chose the best ones?
2. Do you have any questions about your partner's p you disagree with?
3. Can you think of a good title for your partner's pa

> **WRITING** tasks build academic writing skills through step-by-step activities.

7 READING
Cyber-begging

A Pair work Imagine that a stranger asked you for money to help pay off a frivolous debt. Would you help? Tell your partner. Then read the article.

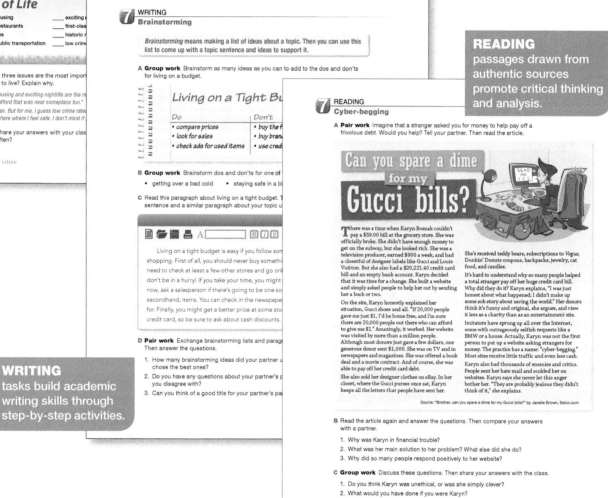

Can you spare a dime for my Gucci bills?

There was a time when Karyn Bosnak couldn't pay a $59.00 bill at the grocery store. She was officially broke. She didn't have enough money to get on the subway, but she looked rich. She was a television producer, earned $900 a week, and had a closetful of designer labels like Gucci and Louis Vuitton. But she also had a $20,221.40 credit card bill and an empty bank account. Karyn decided that it was time for a change. She built a website and simply asked people to help her out by sending her a buck or two.

On the site, Karyn honestly explained her situation, Gucci shoes and all. "If 20,000 people gave me just $1, I'd be home free, and I'm sure there are 20,000 people out there who can afford to give me $1." Amazingly, it worked. Her website was visited by more than a million people. Although most donors just gave a few dollars, one generous donor sent $1,000. She was on TV and in newspapers and magazines. She was offered a book deal and a movie contract. And of course, she was able to pay off her credit card debt. She also sold her designer clothes on eBay. In her closet, where the Gucci purses once sat, Karyn keeps all the letters that people sent her.

She's received teddy bears, subscriptions to *Vogue*, Dunkin' Donuts coupons, backpacks, jewelry, cat food, and candles.

It's hard to understand why so many people helped a total stranger pay off her huge credit card bill. Why did they do it? Karyn explains, "I was just honest about what happened; I didn't make up some sob story about saving the world." Her donors think it's funny and original, she argues, and view it less as a charity than as an entertainment site.

Imitators have sprung up all over the Internet, some with outrageously selfish requests like a BMW or a house. Actually, Karyn was not the first person to put up a website asking strangers for money. The practice has a name: "cyber-begging." Most sites receive little traffic and even less cash. Karyn also had thousands of enemies and critics. People sent her hate mail and scolded her on websites. Karyn says she never let this anger bother her. "They are probably jealous they didn't think of it," she explains.

Source: "Brother, can you spare a dime for my Gucci bills?" by Janelle Brown, Salon.com

B Read the article again and answer the questions. Then compare your answers with a partner.

1. Why was Karyn in financial trouble?
2. What was her main solution to her problem? What else did she do?
3. Why did so many people respond positively to her website?

C Group work Discuss these questions. Then share your answers with the class.

1. Do you think Karyn was unethical, or was she simply clever?
2. What would you have done if you were Karyn?

LESSON B   Information overload   **61**

> **READING** passages drawn from authentic sources promote critical thinking and analysis.

KEEP MOVING UP!
More support is always available – when and where you need it!

The **WORKBOOK** provides extensive practice of grammar and vocabulary as well as additional reading and writing activities.

The **ONLINE WORKBOOK** – a digital version of the Workbook – enables your teacher to provide instant feedback on your work.

The ***PASSAGES* ONLINE VOCABULARY ACCELERATOR** increases the speed and ease of learning new vocabulary through powerful and innovative digital learning techniques.

Plan of **BOOK 1B**

SPEAKING	LISTENING	WRITING	READING
■ Talking about Internet trends ■ Debating whether social networking is a positive or negative influence ■ Giving opinions on modern information technology ■ Discussing potential future technologies	■ Three people talk about social networking ■ A news report describes health problems caused by technology	■ Writing a product or service review	■ "Can you spare a dime for my Gucci bills?": A woman uses the Internet to get money to pay off a frivolous debt
■ Discussing jobs that require creativity ■ Taking a creativity quiz ■ Suggesting new uses for everyday items ■ Talking about creative thinking habits ■ Choosing the inventions that have had the greatest impact on modern life ■ Explaining why new products are invented	■ Three employees explain how their jobs are creative ■ Two descriptions of important business and product ideas	■ Choosing when to begin a new paragraph ■ Writing a composition about a creative or unique person	■ "The Man Who Taught the World to Sing": A profile of the man who invented karaoke
■ Talking about what is typical ■ Discussing what makes you typical or not ■ Discussing the effect of major life changes ■ Giving advice in a role play	■ Three people discuss how they're unique or typical ■ Three people describe how they solved a problem	■ Identifying supporting statements ■ Writing a paragraph with supporting statements	■ "Painting and Problem Solving: Four Lessons": How problem solving and the dynamics of painting are alike
■ Discussing how to handle irritating situations ■ Comparing styles of complaining ■ Role-playing complaints ■ Describing how difficult situations make you feel ■ Stating consumer complaints	■ Two people describe irritating situations ■ A man uses an automated phone menu	■ Writing a message of complaint	■ "Dave Carroll Airs a Complaint": A musician posts music videos to complain about an airline
■ Discussing the results of a survey on ethical behavior ■ Comparing what you would do about different ethical dilemmas ■ Discussing your experiences with unreliable people or services ■ Talking about values that are important to you ■ Explaining what you'd choose if you were given three wishes	■ Two people describe being confronted by an ethical dilemma ■ Three people talk about the values that are most important to them	■ Writing a thesis statement ■ Writing a four-paragraph composition about a happy memory or a regret	■ "New York Honors a Hero": How a construction worker became a hero
■ Describing the benefits and challenges of living abroad ■ Comparing customs between Canada and your country ■ Sharing bad travel experiences ■ Planning a trip with your group	■ Three people talk about their experiences living abroad ■ Two people describe travel mishaps	■ Writing conclusions ■ Writing a composition about living or traveling abroad	■ "Get Yourself Lost": The best way to experience a foreign destination

7 THE INFORMATION AGE

LESSON A ▶ *A weird, wired world*

1 STARTING POINT
Internet trends

A Look at these Internet trends. Choose the ones that affect you.

NOW...

- ☐ Music fans have been given access to nearly unlimited music libraries in "the cloud."
- ☐ Increasingly, information about Internet users is being collected for marketing purposes.
- ☐ Many traditional textbooks have been replaced by online versions.
- ☐ With the development of new online tools, more employees are being allowed to work remotely for part of their workweek.

IN THE FUTURE...

- ☐ Most store purchases will be made by using a mobile device linked to an online account. Cash or credit cards will rarely be used.
- ☐ More and more doctor's examinations are likely going to be done over the Internet.
- ☐ More candidates for employment will be identified, interviewed, and hired online.
- ☐ The Internet is going to be subjected to a greater number of hacker attacks due to the increasing amount of personal information stored online.

B Pair work What did people do before these trends appeared?

"People used to buy CDs, and they put them in CD players to listen to them."

2 VOCABULARY
Technology buzzwords

A Match the terms on the left with the definitions on the right.

1. download ____	a. wireless connection to the Internet
2. app ____	b. a radio or TV show downloadable from the Internet
3. post ____	c. transfer files to your computer or smartphone
4. blog ____	d. harmful software that attacks computers or phones
5. Wi-Fi ____	e. send a short typed message from a cell phone
6. the cloud ____	f. put something on the Internet for others to see
7. podcast ____	g. software that secretly records your online activity
8. spyware ____	h. a program often used on mobile devices
9. text ____	i. large, remote information storage areas on the Internet
10. virus ____	j. an online journal or newsletter, usually of personal opinions

B Pair work Which of these technologies do you have experience with? When do you use them? Why?

"I've been downloading music and videos for years. And if I'm too busy to watch TV, I download podcasts of interesting shows to my smartphone. It's great!"

VOCABULARY PLUS *see page 136*

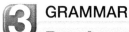

GRAMMAR

Passive of present continuous, present perfect, future

Use the passive for actions where the emphasis is on the object of the action.

Use the passive of the present continuous for ongoing actions.
More employees **are being allowed** to work remotely for part of their workweek.

Use the passive of the present perfect for recently completed actions.
Music fans **have been given** access to nearly unlimited music libraries in "the cloud."

Use *will* + passive or *be going to* + passive for actions that will begin in the future.
Most store purchases **will be made** by using a mobile device linked to an online account.
More and more doctor's examinations **are** likely **going to be done** over the Internet.

GRAMMAR PLUS *see page 118*

A Look at the Starting Point on page 54 again. Can you find more examples of each passive?

B Complete the sentences with the correct passive form of the verb in parentheses. Sometimes more than one answer is possible.

1. Thousands of computers already ___*have been infected*___ (infect) by spyware.

2. Currently, the cloud _____ (utilize) by a large number of businesses.

3. Thousands of blogs _____ (start) on all sorts of topics every day.

4. In coming years, even more fun game apps _____ (develop) for the youth market.

5. Nowadays, teen Internet use _____ (monitor) by concerned parents.

6. These days, podcasts _____ (download) by people of all ages.

7. Many computer viruses _____ (create) by teenagers.

8. In the future, Wi-Fi _____ (make) available in most public places.

LISTENING

Social networking: Different opinions

🔊 **A** Listen to three people's opinions about social networking. What do they mainly use it for?

1. _____   2. _____   3. _____

🔊 **B** Listen again. Choose the correct answers to complete the sentences.

1. Michael believes that social networking at work . . .
   - ☐ a. should be restricted.   ☐ b. makes workers happier.

2. In the case of children, Lisa believes that social networking . . .
   - ☐ a. teaches social skills.   ☐ b. is potentially harmful.

3. Daniel is careful about what he uploads or posts so people won't . . .
   - ☐ a. steal his work.   ☐ b. form a bad opinion of him.

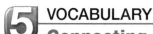

5 Connecting ideas formally

A These expressions connect ideas in different ways. Put them in the correct columns. Sometimes more than one answer is possible.

additionally	as a result	for instance	in fact	nevertheless	similarly
as a matter of fact	for example	furthermore	likewise	on the other hand	therefore

Add information	Compare or contrast	Emphasize	Give an example	Show a result
additionally				

B Choose the appropriate connector to complete the sentences.

1. Tom loves technology; *similarly / for example*, he has the latest cell phone.

2. Many airports offer inexpensive Wi-Fi; *nevertheless / in fact*, at some it's even free.

3. Many of my friends' computers have been damaged by viruses; *nevertheless / therefore*, I am going to update my antivirus software.

4. Some websites aren't reliable; *as a result / likewise*, many people are being misinformed.

5. Few people could have predicted recent advances in Internet technology; *for example / likewise*, predicting the future of the Internet is difficult.

6. Internet identity theft is something very serious; *on the other hand / as a matter of fact*, it can ruin your life.

VOCABULARY PLUS *see page 136*

6 DISCUSSION

Social networking debate

A Pair work Do you think social networking sites are a positive or negative influence? Find a partner who has the same opinion.

B Group work Find a pair who disagrees with you and your partner. Take turns explaining your reasons. Each pair gets a chance to disagree.

"The way I see it, social networking sites are a positive influence because they allow me to have friends all over the world."

"That may be true, but in my opinion, online friends aren't really true friends. In fact, . . ."

Useful expressions		
Expressing opinions	**Disagreeing**	**Giving reasons**
If you ask me, . . .	That may be true, but . . .	That's why . . .
The way I see it, . . .	I see your point, but . . .	The reason for that is . . .

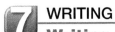

7 WRITING
Writing a product or service review

Writing and posting a product or service review helps other consumers make informed decisions. Most product and service reviews contain similar features.

A Look at the information about product reviews. Then read the review below and select the things the review does. Find examples in the review with a partner.

☐ 1. names the product and explains its use   ☐ 4. suggests how it could be improved

☐ 2. explains where it can be purchased   ☐ 5. states who would find it useful and why

☐ 3. mentions positive features   ☐ 6. gives the exact price

Organize Me XPS is one of the best tools I have used for managing my busy schedule – and I have used many over the years. With this app, I'm able to organize all of my tasks and appointments in one place with just a couple of simple steps. Furthermore, a simple set-up is all it takes to share my plans with others. Having the ability to share my lists and calendars with colleagues and friends like this is extremely useful.

The only drawback some people might find is that it does not have all of the features offered by some of the more expensive productivity apps; nevertheless, it does exactly what I need it to do. In fact, the app's simplicity is its best feature. I just love the simple interface. Although the developers promise that free updates offering new features will be released soon, if you ask me, the low cost makes it a really good value as is.

If you're someone who writes notes on little pieces of paper and then loses them, get this app. It will really boost your productivity. I use it every day – for school, work, and everything else.

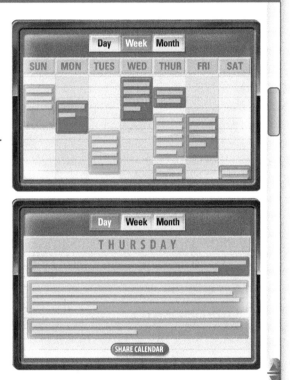

B Use one of these topics or your own idea to write a product or service review.

- technology you purchased
- a game or app you tried
- a restaurant you ate at
- a service you used (dry cleaner, hair salon, mechanic)

C Group work Take turns reading your reviews. Then answer the questions.

1. Whose review is the most interesting and informative? Why?
2. What additional information would you want to know as a consumer?
3. Which reviews would convince you to buy the product or use the service? Which ones would lead you to make a different choice?

LESSON B ► *Information overload*

1 STARTING POINT
Future shock

A Read these comments about technology. Do you agree or disagree?

WHAT'S **Your** TAKE ON TECHNOLOGY?

Joo-chan, Seoul:
"Apps are cool, aren't they? I download lots of them to my smartphone. Wouldn't it be great if phones came loaded with even more apps?"

Ana, São Paulo:
"Isn't it weird how some people use mobile devices constantly? They don't notice anything around them. It's actually dangerous, don't you think?"

Sarah, Los Angeles:
"Don't you think there are too many websites full of misinformation? Shouldn't the government fine sites that contain false information?"

Yang Ming, Taipei:
"Doesn't it seem like kids spend too much time playing violent video games? It makes kids more aggressive, doesn't it?"

B **Pair work** Compare your answers with a partner. Do you think the government should regulate any of these things?

2 VOCABULARY
Forms of communication

A Where do you find these forms of communication? Put them in the correct columns. Then add another expression to each category.

| banner ads | bumper stickers | crawls | infomercials | spam | text messages |
| billboards | bus wraps | fliers | pop-up ads | telemarketing | voice mail |

On television	On the Internet	On the phone	On streets or highways

B **Pair work** Which of the above are the most useful ways of communicating information? The least useful? Do you find any of them annoying?

"Those crawls at the bottom of TV screens aren't useful. It's impossible to read them and pay attention to a show at the same time. Don't you think they're annoying?"

VOCABULARY PLUS *see page 136*

GRAMMAR

Negative and tag questions for giving opinions

Use negative questions or tag questions to offer an opinion and invite someone to react.
Isn't it weird how some people use mobile devices constantly?
Doesn't it seem like kids spend too much time playing violent video games?
Wouldn't it be great if phones came loaded with even more apps?
Shouldn't the government fine sites that contain false information?
Apps are cool, **aren't they**?
It makes kids more aggressive, **doesn't it**?

Use the phrase *don't you think* to form negative or tag questions for opinions.
Don't you think there are too many websites full of misinformation?
It's actually dangerous, **don't you think**?

GRAMMAR PLUS *see page 119*

A Look at the Starting Point on page 58 again. Find the tag questions used by Joo-chan and Yang Ming. Why do they have different endings?

B **Pair work** Turn the statements into negative or tag questions. Then ask and answer the questions. Discuss your answers.

1. It's annoying how often telemarketers call.
2. They should get rid of those banner ads on the Internet.
3. It would be great if there were fewer billboards.
4. It seems like a lot of people are texting while driving.
5. It's sad when people are tricked into losing money by spam messages.
6. There are too many channels on TV these days.

DISCUSSION

It's kind of strange, isn't it?

A **Pair work** Do you agree or disagree with these opinions? Why?

> Millions of people are addicted to online games these days. It's kind of sad, isn't it?

> Wouldn't it be great if the Internet were turned off one day a week to give people a chance to rest?

> Don't you find it annoying that social networking sites sell your personal information to marketers?

> Don't you think a lot of people are being confused by misinformation on the Internet?

> Aren't kids today being exposed to too much information on television and on the Internet?

B **Group work** What other problems are caused by modern information technology? Agree on the three most pressing problems and tell the class.

"Don't you think kids today spend too much time online? Won't their grades and social development suffer because of it?"

"You might be right. But their parents should set limits for them, shouldn't they?"

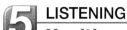

5 LISTENING
Health and technology

 A Listen to a report on health problems caused by technology. Who is the main intended audience? Choose the correct answer.

☐ a. doctors or other health professionals

☐ b. frequent users of technology products

☐ c. designers of computers and mobile devices

B Listen again and complete the chart.

Problem	Symptoms	Advice
texter's thumb		
carpal tunnel syndrome		
gadget addiction		

6 DISCUSSION
Future technologies?

A Read about these technologies. Are any of them available now? Do you think any will be available in the future? Would you like to make use of them? Why or why not?

Technologies of Tomorrow?

You'll never be bored with the color of your clothes or furniture again. With color-changing fabric, you'll be able to select from a wide variety of colors using a remote control, changing colors whenever you want.

Wireless electricity will allow you to do away with chargers, batteries, and cords. Devices and appliances in homes and businesses will run on electricity transmitted wirelessly from a hidden power source.

A life recorder is a small wearable device that will take a video of everything you see, twenty-four hours a day, seven days a week. The sights and sounds of your entire life will be saved for years to come.

B Group work What new technologies are becoming popular? Which ones do you think are useful? What other technologies do you think will be invented in the future?

A **Pair work** Imagine that a stranger asked you for money to help pay off a frivolous debt. Would you help? Tell your partner. Then read the article.

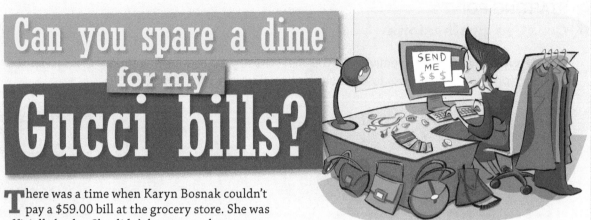

Can you spare a dime for my Gucci bills?

There was a time when Karyn Bosnak couldn't pay a $59.00 bill at the grocery store. She was officially broke. She didn't have enough money to get on the subway, but she looked rich. She was a television producer, earned $900 a week, and had a closetful of designer labels like Gucci and Louis Vuitton. But she also had a $20,221.40 credit card bill and an empty bank account. Karyn decided that it was time for a change. She built a website and simply asked people to help her out by sending her a buck or two.

On the site, Karyn honestly explained her situation, Gucci shoes and all. "If 20,000 people gave me just $1, I'd be home free, and I'm sure there are 20,000 people out there who can afford to give me $1." Amazingly, it worked. Her website was visited by more than a million people. Although most donors just gave a few dollars, one generous donor sent $1,000. She was on TV and in newspapers and magazines. She was offered a book deal and a movie contract. And of course, she was able to pay off her credit card debt.

She also sold her designer clothes on eBay. In her closet, where the Gucci purses once sat, Karyn keeps all the letters that people have sent her.

She's received teddy bears, subscriptions to *Vogue*, Dunkin' Donuts coupons, backpacks, jewelry, cat food, and candles.

It's hard to understand why so many people helped a total stranger pay off her huge credit card bill. Why did they do it? Karyn explains, "I was just honest about what happened; I didn't make up some sob story about saving the world." Her donors think it's funny and original, she argues, and view it less as a charity than as an entertainment site.

Imitators have sprung up all over the Internet, some with outrageously selfish requests like a BMW or a house. Actually, Karyn was not the first person to put up a website asking strangers for money. The practice has a name: "cyber-begging." Most sites receive little traffic and even less cash.

Karyn also had thousands of enemies and critics. People sent her hate mail and scolded her on websites. Karyn says she never let this anger bother her. "They are probably jealous they didn't think of it," she explains.

Source: "Brother, can you spare a dime for my Gucci bills?" by Janelle Brown, Salon.com

B Read the article again and answer the questions. Then compare your answers with a partner.

1. Why was Karyn in financial trouble?

2. What was her main solution to her problem? What else did she do?

3. Why did so many people respond positively to her website?

C **Group work** Discuss these questions. Then share your answers with the class.

1. Do you think Karyn was unethical, or was she simply clever?

2. What would you have done if you were Karyn?

8 PUTTING THE MIND TO WORK
LESSON A ▶ *Exploring creativity*

1 STARTING POINT
Creative professions

A Pair work How much creativity do you think these jobs require? Number them from 1 (most creative) to 4 (least creative). Explain your choices.

____ chef   ____ surgeon   ____ photographer   ____ jazz musician

"I think a chef has to be the most creative. Inventing new dishes requires a lot of creativity."

B Group work Which jobs might be right for these kinds of people? Discuss your answers.

1. someone able to think quickly
2. a person looking for adventure
3. people good with their hands
4. someone needing job security
5. a person trained in music
6. a person with a good voice

"Someone able to think quickly might be a good surgeon. You never know what might go wrong once the operation starts."

2 VOCABULARY
Creative qualities

A What qualities do creative people usually have? Complete the chart with the correct nouns or adjectives.

Noun	Adjective	Noun	Adjective	Noun	Adjective
curiosity	*curious*	innovation			passionate
decisiveness		knowledge		patience	
	determined		motivated		perceptive
	disciplined		original		resourceful

B Pair work Which of the qualities in the chart are most important to your job or studies? Discuss with a partner.

"Well, I'm studying engineering, and we get a lot of assignments, so I have to be very disciplined. It's a very competitive field."

VOCABULARY PLUS *see page 137*

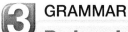

GRAMMAR

Reduced relative clauses

You can shorten a relative clause by dropping the relative pronoun and the verb *be*.
Someone (**who / that is**) **able to think quickly** might be a good surgeon.
A person (**who / that is**) **looking for adventure** could be a private detective.
A person (**who / that is**) **trained in music** might be a good DJ.

You can also drop *who / that* and change the verb to the gerund.
Someone **who / that needs job security** might not want to be a jazz musician.
Someone **needing job security** might not want to be a jazz musician.

In many relative clauses, *who / that* + the verb *have* can be replaced by *with*.
A person **who / that has a good voice** could be a good TV journalist.
A person **with a good voice** could be a good TV journalist.

GRAMMAR PLUS *see page 120*

A Look at the Starting Point on page 62 again. Can you make the reduced relative clauses in part B into full clauses? What verb forms do the full clauses use?

B Rewrite these sentences with reduced relative clauses. Then compare with a partner.

1. Someone who hopes to be a chef should get the proper training.
   Someone hoping to be a chef should get the proper training.

2. Anyone who wants to be an actor needs both talent and luck.

3. A person who works as a comedian is always looking for new ways to make people laugh.

4. People who are clever enough to get inside the mind of a criminal would make good detectives.

5. Anyone who dreams of becoming a champion athlete has to be prepared to do a lot of hard work.

6. Someone who is interested in the latest music trends might be a good DJ.

7. A person who is responsible for a large staff has to be able to be creative with scheduling.

C Complete these sentences using reduced relative clauses and your own ideas.

1. . . . needs to take voice lessons.
   Someone dreaming of becoming a professional singer needs to take voice lessons.

2. . . . should speak English as much as possible.

3. . . . should keep up with current events.

4. . . . doesn't need to have a good speaking voice.

5. . . . should follow the latest trends in clothing.

6. . . . has to study the behavior of animals.

7. . . . usually have a great love of food and eating.

8. . . . will find the job market extremely competitive.

4 DISCUSSION
Creativity quiz

A How creative are you? Complete the quiz.

How **Creative** Are You?

	Always	Sometimes	Rarely	Never
1. Are you a risk taker?	3	2	1	0
2. Are you naturally curious?	3	2	1	0
3. Do you look for opportunities to improve things?	3	2	1	0
4. Are you sensitive to beauty?	3	2	1	0
5. Do you challenge accepted ideas?	3	2	1	0
6. Do you keep an eye out for new fashions and products?	3	2	1	0
7. Do you adapt easily to new situations?	3	2	1	0
8. Do you trust your guesses, intuitions, and insights?	3	2	1	0
9. Are you more interested in the future than in the past?	3	2	1	0
10. Do you have a creative sense of humor?	3	2	1	0

B **Pair work** Add up your score. Then check what your score means below. Do you agree? Why or why not? Tell your partner.

	21-30	11-20	0-10
About You	Because you're open-minded, you like to keep up with the latest trends and innovations. Accepting the status quo bores you. You see mistakes as learning experiences.	You often have good ideas, but you prefer to feel them out with friends before taking action. You're up-to-date with new fashions and products, but unlikely to be the first in your group to try them.	You prefer to stick with the tried-and-true, which helps you feel safe, but you may get left behind in later years. You're content with who you are and what you know.

5 LISTENING
Creativity at work

🔊 **A** Listen to Samira, Alex, and Naomi talking about their occupations. What does each person do?

🔊 **B** Listen again. What do Samira (*S*), Alex (*A*), and Naomi (*N*) say they focus on in their work? Write the correct letter.

_____ 1. helping indecisive clients   _____ 4. solving a wide variety of problems

_____ 2. efficiency   _____ 5. new ideas to replace rejected ones

_____ 3. beating the competition   _____ 6. using old concepts in new ways

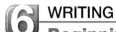

6 WRITING
Beginning new paragraphs

Begin a new paragraph each time you change the focus of your ideas.

A Read this composition. The writer changes focus twice. Indicate with a *P* where the two new paragraphs should begin. Then compare answers with a partner.

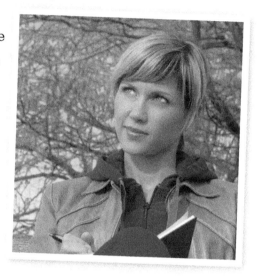

Lucy Gomez is the most creative person I know. She started piano lessons when she was only four years old. At school, she was always creating interesting projects in her art class. When she was only 12 years old, she won a citywide poetry contest. Her parents were very proud of her. Lucy works as a sitcom writer for a popular TV show now. She works with a group of writers, and together they have to think of original ideas for stories. They also have to come up with funny dialogue for the actors on their show, because the actors have to play believable characters that will make the audience laugh. It is not an easy job, but Lucy does it well. She starts work late in the morning and often works until 7:00 or 8:00 at night. Lucy is very curious. She likes to travel and meet new people who have opinions that are different from hers. And she's always noting ideas, drawing quick sketches, and taking photos. She tells me that doing these things helps her turn new experiences into a source of ideas for her work. I always enjoy talking to her and am happy to know someone as knowledgeable and creative as Lucy.

B Brainstorm ideas for a composition about someone who is very creative or who is unique or different in an interesting way. Answer these questions to help you.

1. In what ways is this person special or different?
2. How does this affect his or her life?
3. Would you like to be like this person? Why or why not?

C Write a three-paragraph composition based on your ideas.

D **Pair work** Read your partner's composition and answer these questions.

1. Do the paragraphs start and end where they should?
2. Is the focus of each paragraph clear?
3. Is there any additional information you would like to know that was not included?

1 STARTING POINT
Everyday objects

A Read about these unusual uses of everyday objects. Have you ever used them in these ways?

Three Clever Ideas

1 "I have three cats, which means there's usually a lot of cat fur on my clothes. To get rid of the fur, I wrap my hand in tape, sticky side out. Then I rub the tape over my clothes, and it picks up the fur!"

2 "The zipper was stuck on my favorite jacket. Luckily, my roommate works in fashion, which is great because she knew how to fix it. She just rubbed a drop of olive oil on the zipper."

3 "Tacos can be messy to eat, which is why I wrap them in paper coffee filters. I serve them that way at parties and backyard barbecues. It works great for other messy sandwiches, too!"

B **Group work** Use your imagination to suggest new uses for these everyday items. Decide on the best use for each and share it with the class.

- old newspapers
- a shower curtain
- aluminum foil
- empty shoe boxes
- dental floss
- a hair dryer
- empty jars or cans
- rubber bands

"You can wrap green tomatoes in newspaper to make them ripen more quickly."

2 VOCABULARY & SPEAKING
Exploring possibilities

A Combine the verbs with the nouns to make common expressions.

Verbs			Nouns			
analyze	find	organize	a decision	a problem	a solution	possibilities
explore	make	solve	a mistake	a situation	alternatives	information

analyze a situation, solve a problem, . . .

B **Pair work** Discuss the questions. Then ask your partner more questions using the new vocabulary.

1. When do you make decisions quickly? When do you explore the possibilities first?
2. Who do you talk to when you need to find a solution to a big problem? Why?
3. When was the last time you analyzed a mistake you made? What did you learn from it?

VOCABULARY PLUS *see page 137*

3 GRAMMAR

Non-defining relative clauses as sentence modifiers

You can use non-defining relative clauses with *which* to make a comment about an entire sentence.
I have three cats, **which means there's usually a lot of cat fur on my clothes**.
My roommate is a slob, **which is why I want to get my own apartment**.

GRAMMAR PLUS *see page 121*

A Look at the Starting Point on page 66 again. Can you find more examples of these grammar patterns? How are the commas used?

B Match these statements with the appropriate non-defining clauses. Then compare with a partner and write two similar statements of your own.

1. I want to give away all my old books, __h__

2. I had locked my keys in my car, ____

3. I've been exploring possibilities for natural cleaners, ____

4. My son made a robot costume for himself, ____

5. Our neighbor saves her empty jars for my dad, ____

6. I downloaded a great new app that helps me organize information, ____

7. It's easy to get lost when driving in a new city, ____

8. Adam has bought some expensive software to edit videos, ____

a. which is why you saw me opening it with a coat hanger.

b. which is great since he uses them to store nails and things in his workroom.

c. which is great because I think it's solved my problem of forgetting where I store files.

d. which is why I was wiping lemon juice and salt on those copper pots.

e. which is one reason why GPS systems were developed for cars.

f. which is why he was covered in aluminum foil yesterday.

g. which is strange since there are plenty of free programs that do that well.

h. which means I have to get boxes for them.

4 SPEAKING

Key inventions

A What inventions or discoveries do you think have had the greatest impact on modern life? Make a list.

the cell phone

the television

the airplane

B **Group work** Compare lists with your group.

"I think the cell phone has really affected people's lives. People can talk wherever they are, which means they can always be in touch and save time."

5 LISTENING
Great ideas

A Look at the pictures. What do you know about these products or services? How do you think they were developed?

🔊 **B** Listen to these stories about the invention and development of the products in the photos. Complete the chart.

	Bill Bowerman	Fred Smith
How he got the idea		
The initial reaction to the idea		
What the inventor did in response		

6 DISCUSSION
Making life better

A **Pair work** Why do people create or invent new products? Read this list of reasons and add two more of your own.

- to help protect people's health
- to make business more efficient
- to make daily life easier
- to make life more enjoyable

- to protect the environment
- to save lives
- _____
- _____

B **Group work** Join another pair. Why do you think these things were created or invented? Use the reasons in part A or others of your own.

1. air conditioners
2. artificial sweeteners
3. digital cameras
4. electric knives
5. hybrid cars
6. karaoke machines
7. laptops
8. lie detectors
9. scanners

"I think air conditioners were invented to protect people's health. The summer heat can be deadly for infants and the elderly."

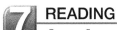

READING

A unique inventor and his invention

A Read the title of the article. What do you think Daisuke Inoue invented?
Then read the article and check your answer.

The Man
Who Taught the World
to Sing

Daisuke Inoue was a drummer in a band near Osaka, Japan, that played versions of famous pop songs. People loved to sing along as the band played, but most of them couldn't carry a tune. Inoue's band had spent years learning how to make the untalented customer sound in tune by adjusting the music to match the customer's voice. The singers, mainly Japanese businessmen out for a night on the town, loved Inoue's unique follow-along style.

In 1971, a loyal client asked Inoue to escort him on a company trip, but Inoue could not attend. He found a solution: he recorded his band's back-up tracks, and then hooked up a car stereo and an amplifier. With this device, Inoue gave birth to the karaoke machine. By the 1980s, *karaoke*, which means "empty orchestra," was a Japanese word that required no translation across the globe.

Unfortunately, Inoue never bothered to patent the world's first karaoke machine, so he lost his chance to become one of Japan's richest men. When asked if he regretted not patenting his invention, 65-year-old Daisuke Inoue confessed, "I'm not an inventor. I am just resourceful. I simply put things that already exist together. Who would consider patenting something like that?"

Inoue's friend Robert Scott Field says, "Some people say he lost 150 million dollars. If it were me, I'd be crying in the corner, but he's a happy guy. I think he's amazed to find that he's touched so many lives." Inoue believes the little box he put together has had a huge social impact, especially in Japan. At weddings and company get-togethers, the karaoke comes out and people relax. It breaks the ice.

Although Inoue spent years in obscurity, in 1999, *Time* magazine called him one of the twentieth century's most influential people, saying he had "helped to liberate the once unvoiced."

Inoue is always getting asked silly questions, but he takes them in stride. "Women approach me all the time and ask if I can help their husbands sing better. I always say that if her husband were any good at singing, he would be making a living at it. He's bad, which means he's just like the rest of us."

Inoue didn't use a modern karaoke machine until he was 59 years old, but his favorite English songs are "Love Is a Many Splendored Thing" and Ray Charles' "I Can't Stop Loving You." "They're easy, which is good because I'm a terrible singer," said Daisuke Inoue, the man who taught the world to sing.

Source: "Mr. Song and Dance Man," by Dr. David McNeill, Sophia University, Tokyo

B Group work Discuss these questions. Then share your answers with the class.

1. What led Daisuke Inoue to create his invention? Do you agree he was only being resourceful, or was he actually an inventor? Explain.

2. Would you have the same attitude as Inoue if you invented something popular and received no compensation? Why or why not?

3. How do you think Inoue "helped to liberate the once unvoiced" both as a drummer in his band and as the inventor of karaoke? Do you think this is a good thing? Explain.

9 GENERALLY SPEAKING

LESSON A ▶ *How typical are you?*

 STARTING POINT
What's typical?

A Read about the "typical" person in Italy and Japan. What information surprised you? Why?

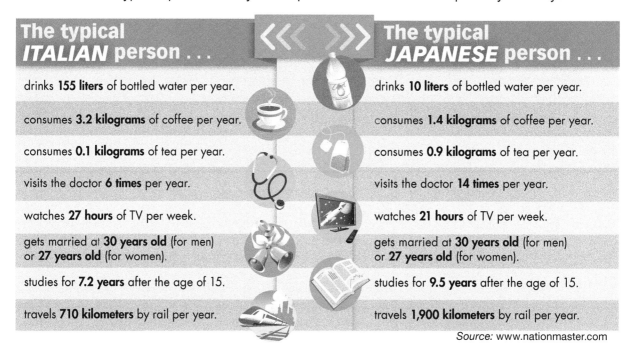

The typical **ITALIAN** person . . .	«« »»	The typical **JAPANESE** person . . .
drinks **155 liters** of bottled water per year.		drinks **10 liters** of bottled water per year.
consumes **3.2 kilograms** of coffee per year.		consumes **1.4 kilograms** of coffee per year.
consumes **0.1 kilograms** of tea per year.		consumes **0.9 kilograms** of tea per year.
visits the doctor **6 times** per year.		visits the doctor **14 times** per year.
watches **27 hours** of TV per week.		watches **21 hours** of TV per week.
gets married at **30 years old** (for men) or **27 years old** (for women).		gets married at **30 years old** (for men) or **27 years old** (for women).
studies for **7.2 years** after the age of 15.		studies for **9.5 years** after the age of 15.
travels **710 kilometers** by rail per year.		travels **1,900 kilometers** by rail per year.

Source: www.nationmaster.com

B Complete these statements. Use information from the chart.

1. Unlike the Japanese, Italians seem to drink a lot of _**bottled water**_____.
2. While the typical _____ person studies until the age of 22, the typical _____ person studies until the age of 24.
3. Both like TV, except that the typical _____ person watches more.
4. In contrast to Italians, the Japanese travel a lot more _____.
5. Both groups are fairly different, except for the age _____.

 SPEAKING
That's just so typical!

A **Pair work** What are typical examples of these things in your hometown?

1. a store 2. a home 3. a job 4. a car 5. a snack food 6. a weekend activity

B **Group work** Join another pair and compare your answers.

"What's a typical store in your hometown?"

"We have something called 'dollar stores.' They have household goods, clothes, toys, and lots of other stuff. And everything's really inexpensive."

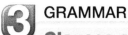

GRAMMAR

Clauses and phrases showing contrast and exception

Use *while*, *unlike*, and *in contrast to* in order to present contrasting information, especially in writing.
While the typical Italian person studies until the age of 22, the typical Japanese person studies until the age of 24.
Unlike the Japanese, Italians seem to drink a lot of bottled water.
In contrast to Italians, the Japanese travel a lot more by rail.

Use *except (that)*, *except (for)*, and *except for the fact (that)* to show an exception.
Both like TV, **except (that)** the typical Italian person watches more.
Italian and Japanese people are fairly different, **except for** the age they get married.
Japanese people typically consume less, **except for the fact that** they drink more tea.

GRAMMAR PLUS *see page 122*

A Look at the Starting Point on page 70 again. Notice the sentences in part B that use phrases with *except*. Which phrase is followed by a clause?

B Here's some information about customs. How are they different in other places? Write sentences showing contrasts and indicating exceptions.

1. When people in the U.S. go to a party, they usually arrive a few minutes late.
   Unlike people in the U.S., most people where I live arrive on time for parties.
2. Most people in Canada have cereal and milk for breakfast some days of the week.
3. Most people in the U.S. who study a foreign language in college choose Spanish.
4. In the U.K., it's common for friends to split the bill at a restaurant.
5. For people in Italy, lunch is the main meal of the day.
6. Women in Spain usually kiss people on both cheeks when they meet.

C Are you typical? Complete these sentences and compare with a partner.

1. Unlike most people where I live, *I don't own a car.*
2. In contrast to most of my friends, . . .
3. While a lot of the people where I live . . .
4. I'm similar to many of my friends, except that . . .

DISCUSSION

Are you typical?

Group work Choose the answer that makes each sentence true for you. Then compare answers with your group. Are you typical in your group?

❶ I need *six or less / seven / eight or more* hours of sleep.
❷ For commuting, I rely mainly on *buses / subways / trains / taxis / a car.*
❸ I tend to eat *healthy / unhealthy snacks* between meals.
❹ I spend the most time with my friends *in person / on the phone / online.*
❺ I button my clothes from the *top down / bottom up.*
❻ A great night out should include a *movie / play / concert / sporting event.*

"Unlike most of the people in my group, I need eight or more hours of sleep or I don't feel rested. Most people in my group need only six hours or less."

5 VOCABULARY
Should I just go with the flow?

A Are these adjectives, verbs, and phrases related to accepting things as they are or to making changes? Put them in the correct columns.

Adjectives	Verbs	Phrases
amenable	accept	be your own person
conservative	conform (to)	fit in
rebellious	confront	follow the crowd
(un)conventional	stand up (to/for)	make waves

Accepting things as they are	Making changes

B Group work Use the expressions in the chart in part A to describe what you think these people might be like. Give examples to explain your ideas.

1. Ed, a guy who gets along with everyone
2. Clarissa, an actor desperate for attention
3. Rob, an assistant at a law firm hoping for a promotion
4. Diana, a leader who wants to change the world

"Ed is probably amenable and does what other people want. I imagine he only confronts people if he really has to and generally follows the crowd."

VOCABULARY PLUS *see page 138*

6 LISTENING & SPEAKING
How are they different?

🔊 **A** Listen to Yoshiko, Diego, and Suzanne talking about their school experiences. Answer the questions.

1. What examples does Yoshiko give for how she is typical? In what way is she different?
2. What are three ways that Diego's life is typical? In what way doesn't he follow the crowd?
3. Does Suzanne give an example of how her life is unconventional? If so, what is it?

🔊 **B** Listen again. Do Yoshiko, Diego, and Suzanne believe they are typical or different from most people their age?

C Pair work Do you tend to go with the flow or be your own person? Discuss these questions.

1. Are your interests similar to those of your friends and family or different? Explain.
2. In what ways do the clothes you wear make you stand out or fit in?
3. How does your taste in music compare to that of other people your age?

Yoshiko in Mexico

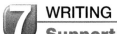

WRITING
Supporting statements

> Supporting statements develop the topic sentence by providing key facts, reasons, or examples.

A Read the paragraph. What's the topic sentence? Underline three supporting statements that develop the main idea in the topic sentence. Then compare your answers with a partner.

http://www.cup.org/myblog/

Unconventionally Cool: Trendspotter Josie Buchier

June 13

My friend Josie Buchier doesn't like to follow the crowd. While most of us are trying our best to fit in with everyone else, Josie likes to be her own person. For instance, she has her own unique sense of fashion, so she likes to buy all her clothes, except for her shoes, in used clothing shops. Her taste in music is also pretty unconventional. Unlike most of my friends, she can't stand pop music. She prefers to listen to Philippine and Andean folk music. She also has a very interesting job. Unlike her old nine-to-five job in a conservative department store, she now works as a trendspotter for an advertising company. This means that she spends her time looking at the latest fashion and entertainment trends among young people. Then she writes reports for her company about what's in style. This makes my unconventional friend a trendsetter that others follow, and that's pretty cool.

[4 comments]

B Finish these statements with information of your own to make topic sentences. Compare with a partner.

1. Generally speaking, most people where I live don't . . .
2. One of my best friends is . . .
3. In general, my friends tend to be . . .

C Choose one of the topic sentences and brainstorm supporting ideas. Then choose at least four supporting statements and write a paragraph.

Generally speaking, most people where I live don't mind making waves. It's their way of . . .

D Pair work Exchange paragraphs and answer these questions.

1. Do all the supporting statements relate to the topic sentence?
2. Do they develop and explain the topic sentence?
3. Do the supporting details fit together in a logical order?
4. What other facts, reasons, or examples could be added?

LESSON B ▶ *Problems and solutions*

1 STARTING POINT
I never used to feel stressed.

A Read Annie's email to her friend. What problems does she have?

To: Adriana Costa
From: Annie Wilson
Subject: Missing you!

Hi Adriana,

How are things back in Cartagena? Are you glad to be home again? Sorry I haven't written lately. I have a lot of new responsibilities at work now, so I've been really stressed. My job didn't use to be so demanding!

I have to say, I miss you. You used to be such a good influence on me! These days, I oversleep. I'm even late for work sometimes! That never used to happen because I knew I had to meet you at the café in the morning. I remember how you would complain about the coffee they served. You used to call it "brown water"!

I'm spending too much money, too. Every time I go to the mall, I see something I want to buy. That's another reason I miss you! I would see some great jacket, but you wouldn't let me buy it. You would always tell me I didn't need it and drag me away!

Also, I have a noisy new roommate, Cindy. All she ever does is gab on her cell! Remember the way we would sit around talking? You always used to make me laugh. I bet that's a big reason I never used to feel stressed like I do now!

Anyway, the weekend will be here soon, so I'm sure I'll feel better then.

Write soon!

Annie

B Pair work What do you think Annie should do about her problems?

"Annie should find another friend to meet at the café in the morning."

2 VOCABULARY
Expressions with *keep* and *stay*

A Match the phrases to make questions. Notice the expressions with *keep* and *stay*.

1. When you're stressed, can you **keep** _e_   a. expenses down?
2. When friends move away, do you **keep / stay** ____   b. up with current events?
3. If you're sleepy while studying, what can you do to **stay** ____   c. connected?
4. What news sources do you read in order to **keep** ____   d. in touch?
5. Do you break the rules or do you **keep / stay** ____   e. things in perspective?
6. How do you save money when you need to **keep** ____   f. awake?
7. Is it important for old friends to **keep / stay** ____   g. out of trouble?

B Pair work Take turns answering the questions. Discuss your answers.

VOCABULARY PLUS *see page 138*

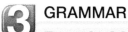

GRAMMAR

Past habitual with *used to* and *would*

Used to and *would* can both be used to describe past habitual actions or situations which are no longer true. However, *would* cannot be used with stative verbs such as *live*, *be*, *have*, or *like*.

You always **used to make** me laugh.
My job **didn't use to be** so demanding!
Remember the way we **would sit** around talking?
I **would see** some great jacket, but you **wouldn't let** me buy it.

GRAMMAR PLUS *see page 123*

A Look at the Starting Point on page 74 again. Make a list of the things that have changed for Annie since Adriana went back to Colombia.

B Complete these sentences with *used to* or *would*. Sometimes more than one answer is possible.

The first year of high school, I wasn't a very good student. I (1) _____ *used to* _____ think school was boring. I remember my classmates (2) _____ go to the library and work on projects or study, but I (3) _____ like to play video games at a friend's house instead. We (4) _____ go right after class, and we (5) _____ spend three or four hours doing that. My parents both (6) _____ have jobs with long hours, so they never knew what time I (7) _____ get home. I thought I was smart, and that I didn't need to study to keep my grades up. But one day, I was asked to go to the principal's office. He said, "You (8) _____ be a great student. Now your grades are terrible. Explain!" That was a real wake-up call. After that, I became serious about school, and I (9) _____ study and finish my homework before playing video games. Now that my kids are in high school, I tell them about all the silly things I (10) _____ do when I was their age.

DISCUSSION

Personal concerns

A **Pair work** These people have had a change in their lives. What positive or negative impacts have these changes had?

Lucas Santos, 25, Curitiba
"Before my wife and I had our first baby, we would go out whenever we wanted. We can't do that now. I didn't use to be a worrier, but I am now."

Britney Majors, 32, Toronto
"Before my promotion, I would eat lunch in the cafeteria because that was all I could afford. Now I have money to go to nice cafés, but I just don't have the time. So, I usually eat at my desk."

Wen Ho Chen, 67, Taipei
"We used to plan on moving in with our son when we retired. But we've changed our minds. We just sold our house, and we're going to travel the world."

B **Group work** Think about a big change in your life. Talk about the positive and negative impacts it had.

"Last year, I was transferred to another department in my company. My new responsibilities are a lot more interesting, but I didn't use to have to work this much."

Different approaches to problem solving

A **Pair work** Read about these three approaches to problem solving. What method do you use? Give examples to support your answer.

What kind of problem solver are you?

Different people solve their problems in different ways. The three main approaches are assertive, meditative, and cooperative. Find out which one best describes you.

▶ **Assertive** people prefer action to talk. When they're faced with a problem, they immediately try to work out a solution.

▶ When **meditative** people have a problem, they sit and think about it, and might even do research. Sometimes, the answer comes to them if they don't act on something right away.

▶ **Cooperative** people think the easiest way to solve a problem is to ask for help. Another person's perspective can help cooperative people come up with solutions.

"I'd say I'm a meditative person. Before I bought my first car, I spent hours doing research on it by myself. It took me forever to decide!"

B Listen to Dominique, Carla, and Wayne talking about their personal concerns. What kind of problem solver is each person?

C Listen again. What are two things each person did to solve their problem?

6 ROLE PLAY

Here's an idea . . .

A Read about these people's problems. What advice would you give each person?

My boss is so demanding. She gives me more work than I can handle.

I can't save money because I always spend it on little things I want but don't really need.

My last job interview went very badly. I always get tongue-tied in front of authority figures.

I'm not enjoying things like I used to. I'm not sure why. Maybe I'm too stressed.

B Role-play each situation. Take turns giving and receiving advice.

"My boss is so demanding. She gives me more work than I can handle."

"Here's an idea. See if your co-workers feel the same way. Maybe you all can talk to the boss about it."

"I guess I could try that."

Useful expressions	
Giving advice	**Receiving advice**
Here's an idea . . .	I guess I could try that.
If I were you, I'd . . .	I just might try that.

A **Pair work** Look at these paintings of the same landscape. How are they different? What effect does this have on what you notice first? Discuss. Then read the article.

Painting and Problem Solving: *FOUR LESSONS*

Earlier this month I escaped the office for a weeklong painting retreat in the woods of Door County, Wisconsin. While working amidst the awe-inspiring fall colors, it occurred to me that the dynamics of painting and problem solving have a lot in common. I returned home not only with newly polished painting skills but also a fresh perspective on managing problems. I learned four lessons while painting:

1 **How you see things depends on your line of sight.** When painting a landscape, countless choices are yours. For starters, you can choose where to place the horizon and what you eliminate from the actual setting. If the existing landscape is cluttered, for instance, you can exclude elements that detract from your focal point. Likewise, in problem solving, getting caught up in the clutter diminishes your ability to reach your desired result. Choose instead to focus on the bigger picture.

2 **People can see the same landscape and represent it in totally different ways.** One day I sat with two other painters in a microclimate with magnificent sugar maples. Much to my surprise, our final paintings were totally different. A similar phenomenon occurs in problem solving: Any number of people can arrive at the same situation with different ideas, skills, or resources. They can also have different designs on the end result. In this way, respecting where others are coming from is critical to problem solving.

3 **When light is shined on a subject, you can explore what lies in the shadows.** It can be harder to paint landscapes on cloudy days. The various forms and contrasts are less clear, and it's difficult to explore what lies in the shadows. When the sun is shining, however, the distinctions between objects are clearly visible and what lies in the shadows is revealed. The same goes for problem solving: When you shine a light on an issue, you see everything more clearly, including what opportunities or threats exist in the shadows.

4 **Collaborating with people at different levels can foster appreciation for diverse ideas and perspectives.** At the retreat, there were painters at every level, from first-timers to fine artists. I learned something from each one, particularly when our group came in from the woods and worked together in the studio. I opened myself up to others' unique observations and feedback, and ultimately felt more energized and creative. Additionally, I was struck by our instructor's capacity to calibrate her critiques to our individual skill levels. Similarly, in problem solving, it's important to meet others where they are, not where you might want them to be.

Odds are there is a problem on your desk today. How might even one of these four lessons help you brush up your problem-solving skills?

Source: "4 Ways to Brush Up Your Problem-Solving Skills," by Barbara T. Armstrong

B **Group work** Discuss these questions. Then share your answers with the class.

1. In what way is it helpful to avoid paying attention to details when solving a problem?

2. How are the second and fourth lessons in the article similar?

3. What do you think the author means by "shine a light on an issue"? How is this helpful?

4. How can the lessons from the article help you solve one of your own problems?

SELF-ASSESSMENT

How well can you do these things? Choose the best answer.

I can . . .	Very well	OK	A little
▶ Describe how information technology has changed people's lives (Ex. 1)	☐	☐	☐
▶ Describe how new technologies will change people's lives (Ex. 2)	☐	☐	☐
▶ Understand the main points of a phone conversation about personality types (Ex. 3)	☐	☐	☐
▶ Describe my personality type (Ex. 3)	☐	☐	☐
▶ Describe and compare typical behavior of parents and teenagers (Ex. 4)	☐	☐	☐

Now do the corresponding exercises. Was your assessment correct?

1 DISCUSSION
How things have changed!

A Think about how information technology has changed in the past few years. How have people's shopping habits, hobbies, and social lives been affected?

B Pair work Compare your answers with a partner.

"Video games used to be low-tech and expensive. Some games used to be available on the Internet, but few people would play them. Now, a lot of people play video games online. I think they've been greatly improved, and many are fairly cheap."

"Yeah, I think so, too. But too much time is spent playing them. My whole family is addicted – even my grandmother plays! She used to think video games were a waste of time when I played them as a kid."

2 DISCUSSION
What next?

A Pair work What do you think will happen in the next 10 years as a result of new technologies in these areas?

1. communication
2. education
3. entertainment
4. finance
5. medicine
6. sports

B Group work Compare your predictions in groups.

"Ten years from now, I think cell phones will be used by everyone. They'll even be used at work instead of office phones. What do you think?"

3 LISTENING & SPEAKING
Team roles: The perfect "STEAM" team

 A Listen to the phone conversation between Tony and Annie. What is Tony's agency doing? Choose the correct answer.

- ☐ a. They're exploring the possibilities of using cell phones in advertising.
- ☐ b. They're analyzing the effectiveness of their advertisements.
- ☐ c. They're working to improve a company's image.

B Listen again. Match the roles on the left with the personality types on the right.

Role	Personality type
1. Solver _*d*_	a. disciplined
2. Team manager ____	b. patient
3. Explorer ____	c. passionate
4. Analyst ____	d. creative
5. Motivator ____	e. resourceful

C Pair work Look at the roles again. Which role do you think you would be best at or would enjoy most? Why? Compare your ideas with a partner.

"I think I'd probably be best in an Explorer role. I'm pretty resourceful. What about you?"

"I'm a person with a lot of patience, but I'm not that creative. I'm more of a Team manager type."

4 SPEAKING
That's so typical!

A Complete this chart with your opinions about typical parents and teenagers.

	The typical parent	The typical teenager
What are some of their concerns?		
What is their most valued possession?		
How much time do they spend with friends?		
What do they use the Internet for?		
What do they like to do on vacation?		

B Write at least four sentences contrasting the typical parent with the typical teenager. Then compare with a partner.

"Generally, the typical teenager is concerned about friends, while the typical parent is concerned about his or her children."

10 THE ART OF COMPLAINING
LESSON A ▶ *That really bugs me!*

1 STARTING POINT
Everyday annoyances

A Have you ever had problems similar to these? Do you agree or disagree with these comments? Why?

"The thing that I hate is when kids ride their scooters on the sidewalk."

"One thing that bothers me is when my friends don't show up on time for things."

"Something that bugs me is people who take up two seats on a crowded bus."

"The thing I can't stand is co-workers who leave their cell phones ringing on their desks."

B **Group work** Look at the situations in part A. Would you complain, or would you be quietly annoyed? Why?

2 LISTENING & SPEAKING
It really irks me!

🔊 **A** Listen to Jane and Kyle talking about irritating situations. What bothered each person?

🔊 **B** Listen again. Discuss the questions.

1. Whose situation do you think was more annoying, Jane's or Kyle's?
2. Who do you think handled the situation better, Jane or Kyle?
3. How would you have reacted in each situation?

3 GRAMMAR

Relative clauses and noun clauses

A relative clause can occur in the subject or the object of a sentence.
Something **that bugs me** is people **who take up two seats on a crowded bus**.
The thing **(that)** I can't stand is co-workers **who / that leave their cell phones ringing on their desks**.

Some sentences use a relative clause and a noun clause beginning with a question word such as *when*.
The thing **(that)** I hate is **when kids ride their scooters on the sidewalk**.
One thing **that bothers me** is **when my friends don't show up on time for things**.

GRAMMAR PLUS *see page 124*

A Look at the Starting Point on page 80 again. Which clauses are relative clauses? Which are noun clauses?

B Pair work Complete the sentences with your own opinions. Then discuss them with a partner.

1. One thing that irks me about my neighbors is . . .
   when they park too close to my car.
2. Something that bothers me about my friends is . . .
3. If I'm riding in a car, something that irritates me is . . .
4. The thing that aggravates me most is a friend . . .
5. The thing that annoys me about people talking on cell phones is . . .
6. . . . is one thing that bothers me at home.

4 VOCABULARY

That drives me up the wall!

A Combine the verbs with the phrases. How many combinations can you make? How are their meanings different?

Verbs	Phrases		
drive	on someone's nerves	someone mad	someone upset
get	someone crazy	someone sick	someone's blood boil
make	someone down	someone up the wall	under someone's skin

B Group work How do these things make you feel? Discuss these situations using the expressions in part A.

1. people laughing at their own jokes
2. vending machines that "steal" your money
3. finding empty ice cube trays in the freezer
4. people eating on public transportation
5. airlines not serving food on long flights

"The thing that drives me crazy is when people laugh at their own jokes, and they're not funny!"

VOCABULARY PLUS *see page 139*

DISCUSSION
Polite complaints

A Which of these descriptions fits you best? Give examples to support your answer.

I very rarely complain.

a silent sufferer

I only complain if I absolutely have to.

a calm, collected type

I complain because it's my right.

an activist

I complain about every little thing.

a whiner

"I guess I'm a silent sufferer. For example, I never complain in a restaurant, even if the food is awful."

"You don't? Bad food in a restaurant really annoys me. I always complain! I mean, why should I pay for terrible food? I guess I must be an activist."

B **Pair work** What would you do or say in these situations? Compare your answers.

1. A taxi driver is playing the radio loudly while you are trying to make a phone call.
2. Your neighbor's young son tore up all the flowers in your garden.
3. You see someone littering in a public park.

"If the taxi driver were playing the radio very loudly, I think I'd just speak louder. I probably wouldn't say anything to the driver. But I wouldn't give him a very good tip either."

ROLE PLAY
I hate to mention this, . . .

A **Pair work** Use the language in the box to create polite complaints for each situation. Then take turns acting out your complaints for the class.

1. You've been waiting in line for a long time, and someone suddenly cuts in front of you.
2. You've had a party, and one friend is still at your home long after everyone else has left. It's driving you up the wall because it's really late, and you need to get up early.
3. After you've been waiting patiently for your food for an hour, the waiter brings you the wrong order.
4. Every time you go out with your friend, she asks you to hold her belongings because she doesn't carry a bag. It's really beginning to get on your nerves.

Useful expressions

Complaining to strangers
Excuse me, but . . .
I'm sorry, but . . .

Complaining to friends/neighbors
I hate to mention this, but . . .
I'm sorry to bring this up, but . . .

B **Group work** Which complaints were the most effective? Which were the most polite?

WRITING
Messages of complaint

> Writing an effective message of complaint is a powerful way to solve an ongoing problem with a product or service.

A Match the information to the points in the email.

Writing an effective message of complaint
An effective message of complaint about a purchase ...

1. contains a clear subject line.
2. describes the product or service clearly.
3. explains the problem in detail.
4. mentions a receipt or other evidence.
5. explains exactly what you want.
6. provides contact information.

To: customerservice@phonegrp.cup.org

From: JM1990@cup.org

Subject: Damaged product —— 1

Dear Sir or Madam:

Last month, I ordered a smartphone, model number VG25S, from your website. When it arrived, I discovered that it was broken. The case was damaged, and the display screen was cracked.

At my own expense, I returned the phone to your service department over a month ago. I still have not received a replacement, nor has a customer service representative contacted me.

I have my credit card bill to prove I paid for this purchase, a one-year warranty, and a receipt from the post office. Therefore, I would like to receive a new phone as soon as possible.

Please call or email me about this matter. I look forward to your reply and hope you will handle this matter promptly.

Sincerely,

John Montgomery
101 Bee Tree Road
Encino, CA 91426
Phone: 310-555-2934

B Write an email complaining about one of these situations or one of your own.

- Your tablet came with the wrong battery charger, but you didn't notice until you brought it home. You called the store, and they refused to replace it.

- You bought airplane tickets in advance, but the airline had overbooked the flight, and you couldn't get on the plane.

C **Pair work** Take turns reading your emails. Did your partner follow all the steps for writing an effective message of complaint?

LESSON B ▶ *Let's do something about it!*

1 STARTING POINT
Why don't they do something about it?

A How many of these problems have you experienced? Compare with a partner.

"Overcrowded buses really make me mad. I wonder why they don't have more buses at rush hour."

"Umbrellas are so poorly made these days. I don't know why they always break in the wind."

"My cell phone never works around here. I can't understand why the reception is so bad."

For service in English, press 1.

"Automated phone menus drive me crazy. What I don't get is why companies don't have people answer their phones."

"The clothes in those shops are unbelievably expensive. How anyone can afford them is beyond me."

"The college course I want is really popular. My big concern is whether I'll be able to get into the class."

B Pair work Which of the problems in part A bother you the most? Explain.

"Broken umbrellas definitely bother me the most. That happened to me just the other day."

"You can say that again. I just hate it when that happens."

Useful expressions

Agreeing and showing sympathy
I know (exactly) what you mean.
Yeah, I hate that too.
You can say that again.

2 LISTENING
If this is correct, say, "Yes."

A Have you ever had problems with automated phone menus? What happened?

◄)) **B** Listen to Gabriel using an automated phone menu. Is he successful? Choose the best summary.

☐ a. He completed his business successfully and will pick up his prescription this evening.

☐ b. He can't fill his prescription because the machine didn't recognize what he said.

☐ c. His pronunciation is so poor that the system didn't understand anything he said.

◄)) **C** Listen again. Answer the questions.

1. What's the name of the store?
2. What is his prescription number?
3. What is his phone number?
4. What time does he want to pick up his prescription?

84 **UNIT 10** The art of complaining

GRAMMAR
Simple and complex indirect questions

Simple indirect questions use statement word order and begin with expressions such as
I wonder, I'd like to know, or *I can't understand*.

Why don't they have more buses at rush hour?   I wonder why **they don't have** more buses at rush hour.

Complex indirect questions also use statement word order. In addition, they begin or end with
clauses or phrases with *be*.

Will I be able to get into the class?   **My big concern is** whether I'll be able to get into the class.
How can anyone afford them?   How anyone can afford them **is beyond me**.

GRAMMAR PLUS *see page 125*

A Look at the Starting Point on page 84 again. Can you find more indirect questions? Which ones are simple indirect questions? Which are complex?

B Rewrite these questions using the words in parentheses. Then compare answers with a partner.

1. Will airlines ever stop losing passengers' luggage? (I wonder . . .)
   I wonder if airlines will ever stop losing passengers' luggage.
2. How do I correct a mistake on my phone bill? (I'd like to know . . .)
3. Why can't I use my cell phone in an elevator? (The thing I don't get is . . .)
4. How can I get tickets to sold-out concerts? (I want to find out . . .)
5. When will the government deal with global warming? (I'd like to know . . .)
6. Why do people complain so much? (. . . is something I can't understand.)

VOCABULARY & SPEAKING
I'm totally baffled!

A Look at these words that describe feelings. Put them in the correct columns.

annoyed   confused   depressed   enraged   humiliated   insulted   mystified   stunned
baffled   demoralized   discouraged   frustrated   infuriated   irritated   saddened

Confused feelings	Angry feelings	Sad feelings
baffled	annoyed	

B **Pair work** Complete the sentences with your own information. Then discuss your answers with a partner.

1. I'm totally baffled by . . .
2. I get so infuriated when . . .
3. I always get discouraged when . . .
4. I wouldn't be demoralized even if . . .
5. I remember feeling stunned when . . .
6. I would feel insulted if . . .

"I'm totally baffled by people who can speak a lot of languages. How do they remember so many different words and grammar rules?"

VOCABULARY PLUS *see page 139*

5 DISCUSSION
A word to the wise

A **Pair work** Read the advice about how to avoid consumer problems. Can you add any more ideas to the list?

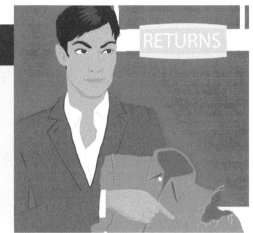

Buyer **Beware!**
SMART ADVICE FOR SMART SHOPPERS

- Buy from a reputable company.
- Make sure there's a guarantee.
- Examine your purchases before you buy.
- Do some comparison shopping.
- Find out about the return policy.
- Find out how the item should be cared for.

B **Group work** Discuss a time when you had a problem with something you bought. Would the advice in part A have helped you?

"I bought some really expensive luggage last month, and I was enraged when, after just a week, one of the wheels came off."

"Oh, you're kidding. Did you take it back to the store?"

"Yes, but they told me I couldn't return it because I'd bought it on sale. I should have asked about their return policy . . ."

Useful expressions

Sympathizing
Oh, you're kidding.
That's ridiculous.
What a pain.

6 ROLE PLAY
I'd like to return this.

A Read the store returns policy in part B. Is there a similar policy at the stores where you shop?

B **Pair work** Take turns role-playing a customer and a clerk at a returns counter. Use the returns policy and the situations below.

STORE RETURNS POLICY: All items must be in good condition and accompanied by a receipt. No cash refunds; store credit only. No items returned after two weeks unless under warranty. No return of items purchased on sale or with coupons.

Situation 1	**Situation 2**	**Situation 3**
• T-shirt	• laptop	• camera
• have receipt	• receipt at home	• lost receipt
• shrank after washing	• defective	• not very user-friendly
• now too small	• still under warranty	• want to exchange

"I'd like to return this T-shirt, please. I can't understand why it shrank after I washed it."

"I wonder whether you followed the washing instructions properly."

"I certainly did!"

"That's fine, then. May I see your receipt, please?"

The power of one voice

A **Pair work** What steps would you take if someone damaged one of your valuable possessions? Discuss with a partner. Then read the article and find out what Dave Caroll did. Did he take any of the steps you discussed?

Dave Carroll Airs a Complaint

Dave Carroll was ready to quit his 20-year career as an independent musician. Then, an airline broke his guitar and changed his life.

The airline wouldn't budge on Dave's request for $1,200 in flight vouchers to cover repairs to his $3,500 Taylor guitar. When he got "The Final No!" email after nine months of negotiations, he wrote back to say he wasn't without options.

Dave said that if he were a lawyer, he might have sued the airline, but as a songwriter, he had other tools at his disposal. He vowed to write two or three songs, make a music video for each one, and post them on YouTube.

"After months of feeling frustrated and angry about the ordeal, for the first time I felt empowered, as though a weight had been lifted from me. I changed gears from someone who *wanted* something to someone who was going to *do* something."

His goal was to reach one million views in the next year. Four days after he posted the first video, he hit a million views. The airline called him a day after the video was released to offer the same $1,200 in flight vouchers he'd asked for previously, plus an extra $1,200 in cash. Carroll refused the offer. His goal had moved beyond compensation to sharing his story and improving conditions for all travelers.

His newfound fame has revived his music career. His trilogy of songs about his experience has had approximately 15 million YouTube views. He's done media interviews and given speeches around the world. Ironically, the airline now uses his videos to train staff and pays him a license fee to do so, at his request.

He's also helped launch a website, Gripevine.com, for people to air problems and get them fixed. Companies now know that a disgruntled customer's view can go viral in a heartbeat and reach an immense audience. As Dave tells businesses, it's vital for companies to listen and learn.

Source: "Dave Carroll is still having problems with airlines," by Ellen Roseman, The Toronto Star

B **Pair work** Number the events in the correct order. Write *X* for the two events that are not part of Dave's story. Then take turns telling the story in your own words.

____ a. Dave decided to use his songwriting skills to address his problem in a creative way.

____ b. Dave rejected the airline's offer even though they'd doubled his original request.

____ c. Dave sued the airline for the amount of money it would cost to repair his guitar.

____ d. Dave's guitar was damaged by an airline, and they refused to compensate him.

____ e. The airline offered Dave what he wanted after he posted his song on YouTube.

____ f. Dave gave up on his dreams of becoming a musician after 20 years in the business.

____ g. Dave helped start an online consumer group and relaunched his career.

C **Group work** Discuss these questions. Then share your answers with the class.

1. What made Dave finally feel empowered during his struggle with the airline?

2. In what ways has social media given ordinary people more power? Give examples.

11 VALUES

LESSON A ► *How honest are you?*

1 STARTING POINT
What would you do?

A Look at the situations and people's responses. What would you do?

If you accidentally damaged a parked car in a parking lot . . .

"If the owner weren't around, I'd leave a note with my phone number."

"I wouldn't leave a note if the owner weren't around."

If you found out your co-worker got the job using false credentials . . .

"I would keep it a secret only if I liked my co-worker."

"I would keep it a secret unless my boss asked me directly about it."

If you found some money on the street . . .

"I wouldn't try to return it unless it were a large amount."

"Even if I were really broke, I'd give the money to the police."

B **Pair work** Now read these statistics. Do you find them surprising? Why or why not?

Of the people surveyed . . .

62% would never fail to report damaging a parked car even if nobody were present.

48% think it is unacceptable to use false credentials on a job application.

18% wouldn't keep money they found on the street.

58% would never illegally avoid paying the fare on public transportation.

25% think it's never **OK** to exceed the speed limit while driving.

Source: British Election Study at the University of Essex, Economic and Social Research Council

2 LISTENING
Finders keepers

🔊 Listen to Aaron and Leanne talking about finding something. Are these statements true or false, or does the person not say? Choose the correct answer.

	True	False	Doesn't say
1. Aaron's son wanted to keep the wallet and spend the money.	☐	☐	☐
2. Aaron's son received a thank-you card as a reward.	☐	☐	☐
3. The owner of the book probably didn't care much about it.	☐	☐	☐
4. Leanne will probably return the book.	☐	☐	☐

GRAMMAR

Present unreal conditional with *unless, only if,* and *even if*

Unless clauses include exceptions that would change the speaker's decision.
I **wouldn't** try to return it **unless** it **were** a large amount.
I **would** keep it a secret **unless** my boss **asked** me directly about it.

Only if clauses stress the condition for the result.
I **would** keep it a secret **only if** I **liked** my co-worker.

Even if clauses are followed by unexpected results.
Even if I **were** really broke, **I'd** give the money to the police.

GRAMMAR PLUS *see page 126*

A Look at the Starting Point on page 88 again. Look at the responses to the first situation. Are they different in meaning? If so, how?

B Choose the words that are true for you. Then complete the sentences.

1. If a cashier undercharged me, I (would)/ *wouldn't* tell him *if* /(even if) . . .
   If a cashier undercharged me, I would tell him even if it were a small difference.

2. I *would / wouldn't* borrow a lot of money from a friend *only if / unless* . . .

3. I *would / wouldn't* return a gift I'd received to the store *if / unless* . . .

4. I *would / wouldn't* "temporarily borrow" an unlocked bicycle on the street *only if / even if* . . .

5. I *would / wouldn't* report my friend for skipping work *only if / unless* . . .

 VOCABULARY & SPEAKING

It's a little unethical.

A These words describe people's ethics and attitudes. Which prefixes give them the opposite meaning? Put the words in the correct columns.

acceptable	approving	fair	legal	rational	scrupulous
agreeable	ethical	honest	logical	responsible	trustworthy

dis-	il-	ir-	un-
			unacceptable

B **Pair work** Use the vocabulary words in part A to discuss these questions.

1. Would you ever make an international call from work to save money?
2. Would you ever play a practical joke on your friends?
3. Would you ever tell a friend with a terrible new haircut that you think it's fantastic?

VOCABULARY PLUS *see page 140*

5 DISCUSSION
Ethical dilemmas

A Read these situations. What would you do?

What Would You Do ?

1 You've had plans for several weeks to visit your aunt. The day before, your friend invites you to a really great party the same night.

- Would you cancel your original plans?
- If so, would you tell the truth or "a white lie" about why you were canceling?
- Would you cancel your plans even if you knew your aunt were looking forward to seeing you?

2 You're at a convenience store, and you see someone shoplifting a can of soup.

- Would you tell the clerk?
- What if the shoplifter were a woman with a small child?
- Would it make a difference if the shoplifter looked dangerous?

3 You work full-time during the day. You're also a part-time student in an evening course, so you have a student ID card. Businesses all over town give discounts to students.

- Would you use your student ID to get the cheaper prices?
- What if you earned a high salary at your job?
- Would it make a difference if you were buying from a major chain store or from a small mom-and-pop business?

B Group work Share your answers and give reasons for each. Then agree on the best course of action for each situation.

"Unless it were a special occasion for my aunt, I might leave a little early so I could get to the party before it ended."

6 DISCUSSION
Too good to be true

A Which of these situations seem reliable? Choose those that seem legitimate.

☐ 1. A website offers free international phone service.

☐ 2. A company sends you an email asking you to confirm your credit card details online.

☐ 3. Someone on the street asks you to sign a petition that requires your address and phone number.

☐ 4. A television ad offers a set of knives worth $300 for just $75.

B Pair work Discuss these or similar situations. Share your own experiences or those of people you know.

"I once bought a kitchen appliance that I saw advertised on TV. The price was really good, and it worked well at first, but after a few weeks, it broke."

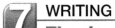

WRITING
Thesis statements

> A topic sentence states the main idea of a single paragraph. A thesis statement introduces the topic of a composition. It is often located at the beginning or end of the first paragraph.

A Read the composition and choose the best thesis statement from the choices below. Then, write a *T* where you think the thesis statement should appear.

1. *I've made some bad decisions.*
2. *We learn a lot from the decisions we make.*
3. *I have good and bad memories of old friendships.*

When I'm faced with a decision that puts my ethics on the line, I think about what similar situations in the past have taught me. In my life, I've made both good and bad choices.

One of my good decisions resulted in a casual friend becoming a very close friend. A college classmate gave me a lottery ticket for my birthday. As she gave it to me, she joked that if I won, I should split the prize with her. I ended up winning $500. At the time, I was saving for a new tablet, and with the $500, I had enough money. I considered not telling my friend that I'd won. But I felt dishonest and disloyal, and I gave her half. I'll always be glad I did, and I wouldn't do it any differently today, even if I really needed all the money. Today, she is still one of my best friends.

One of my bad decisions ruined a friendship. A former classmate wanted a job with my company and asked me to recommend her. I knew she didn't have very good work habits. I told her I would do it only if she promised to work hard. She was hired, but three months later, she was fired because my boss thought she was irresponsible and her work was unacceptable. I was fairly new at the company myself, and my company is still a little unsure about trusting my judgment now. I don't have much to do with her these days.

I believe that good and bad decisions are a part of everyone's personal development. Is it possible to learn from those experiences? I think it is because even the bad ones help to prepare you for the future.

B Write a four-paragraph composition about a happy memory or a regret. Follow these guidelines.

1st paragraph: Introduce your topic in the paragraph. Begin or end the paragraph with your thesis statement.

2nd paragraph: Write about a decision you would make again.

3rd paragraph: Write about a decision you would make differently.

4th paragraph: End with a strong conclusion.

Your thesis statement . . .
- *should contain a single idea.*
- *should be neither too general nor too specific.*
- *should unify all the paragraphs.*
- *can be improved as you write.*

C **Group work** Take turns reading your compositions. Is the thesis statement too general? Does it need to be improved?

STARTING POINT

I wish . . .

A Read these messages. Match each message with one of the values below.

a. careful spending   c. perseverance   e. career advancement

b. concern for others   d. good family relations   f. good cross-cultural relations

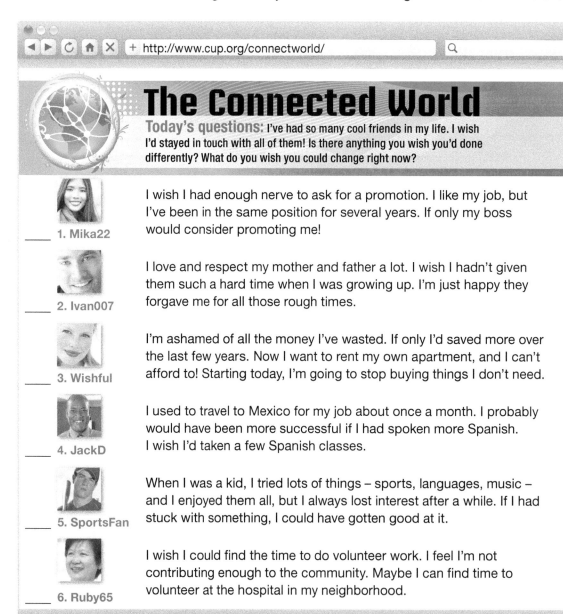

http://www.cup.org/connectworld/

The Connected World

Today's questions: I've had so many cool friends in my life. I wish I'd stayed in touch with all of them! Is there anything you wish you'd done differently? What do you wish you could change right now?

_____ **1. Mika22**
I wish I had enough nerve to ask for a promotion. I like my job, but I've been in the same position for several years. If only my boss would consider promoting me!

_____ **2. Ivan007**
I love and respect my mother and father a lot. I wish I hadn't given them such a hard time when I was growing up. I'm just happy they forgave me for all those rough times.

_____ **3. Wishful**
I'm ashamed of all the money I've wasted. If only I'd saved more over the last few years. Now I want to rent my own apartment, and I can't afford to! Starting today, I'm going to stop buying things I don't need.

_____ **4. JackD**
I used to travel to Mexico for my job about once a month. I probably would have been more successful if I had spoken more Spanish. I wish I'd taken a few Spanish classes.

_____ **5. SportsFan**
When I was a kid, I tried lots of things – sports, languages, music – and I enjoyed them all, but I always lost interest after a while. If I had stuck with something, I could have gotten good at it.

_____ **6. Ruby65**
I wish I could find the time to do volunteer work. I feel I'm not contributing enough to the community. Maybe I can find time to volunteer at the hospital in my neighborhood.

B **Pair work** Which person in part A are you most like? Which of the values are the most important? What are some of the values you learned when you were growing up?

"I'm similar to Ruby65. I really think it's important to show concern for other people. As I was growing up, my parents also taught me the importance of . . ."

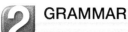

GRAMMAR

Wishes and regrets

For wishes about the present and future, use *wish* + simple past, past continuous, or *could* / *would* + verb.
I **wish** I **had** enough nerve to ask for a promotion.
I **wish** I **could find** the time to do volunteer work.

For regrets about the past, use *wish* + past perfect.
I **wish** I**'d taken** a few Spanish classes.
I **wish** I **hadn't given** my parents such a hard time when I was growing up.

For regrets about the past, use *if* + past perfect and *could* / *would have* + past participle.
If I **had stuck** with something, I **could have gotten** good at it.

For strong wishes about the present or future, or for strong regrets about the past, use *if only*.
If only clauses are often used without a main clause.
If only my boss **would consider** promoting me!

GRAMMAR PLUS *see page 127*

A Look at the Starting Point on page 92 again. Which sentences express regrets about the past? Which ones describe wishes for the present or future?

B Rewrite these statements using the words in parentheses. Compare answers with a partner. Are any of the sentences true for you?

1. I can't find the time to exercise. (I wish . . .)
   I wish I could find the time to exercise.
2. My grades weren't very good last semester. (If only . . .)
3. I don't know how to dance very well. (I wish . . .)
4. I didn't apply for that interesting job at work. (I wish . . .)
5. I'm feeling very stressed these days. (I wish . . .)
6. I never learned how to swim when I was a child. (If only . . .)
7. I gave away my old guitar last year. (If only . . .)
8. I watched too much TV and didn't read enough when I was a kid. (If only . . .)

C Complete these sentences with your own wishes or regrets and add extra information. Then compare answers with a partner.

1. If only I had enough money to . . . ! Then I wouldn't . . .
   If only I had enough money to buy a motorcycle!
   Then I wouldn't have to take the bus to class.
2. I wish I could find the time to . . . . If I could, I would . . .
3. I wish I had learned how to . . . when I was a kid. If I had, I'd . . .
4. If only I knew how to . . . . Then I could . . .
5. I wish my friends would . . . so that . . .
6. If only I had listened to my parents when they told me . . . because . . .
7. I wish they would pass a law that says . . . . If they did, . . .
8. If only I had the courage to . . . . Then I would . . .

3 VOCABULARY & SPEAKING
Personal values

A What words describe people's values? Complete the chart with the correct noun or adjective.

Noun	Adjective	Noun	Adjective	Noun	Adjective
compassion	*compassionate*		indifferent	selfishness	
	discreet	kindness		sensitivity	
generosity		resilience			tender
	honest		respectful		tolerant

B Pair work Which three values do you think are most important? Decide with a partner. Give your reasons.

"We thought generosity, tolerance, and honesty were most important. Generosity is an important value because if you help people, they might help you one day. Tolerance matters because . . ."

VOCABULARY PLUS *see page 140*

4 LISTENING & SPEAKING
Three important values

 A Listen to these on-the-street interviews. What values do these people think are important? Number the values in the order you hear them.

____ honesty   ____ privacy   ____ respect

 B Listen again. Whose answer did you agree with the most? Why do you think so?

"I'd say I agreed with the first woman the most. If you're not honest, you'll only get yourself into trouble. Plus, telling the truth is the right thing to do."

5 SPEAKING
Grant me a wish.

A If you could have three wishes, what would they be? Make a list.

B Pair work Compare your wishes with a partner. Then share your answers with the class.

"My first wish would be for my family to stay healthy and happy. Second, I would wish for more peace in the world. For my last wish, . . ."

A Pair work Read the title and the first paragraph of the news article. What would you have done if you were Wesley Autrey? Discuss, and then read the article.

NEW YORK HONORS A HERO

It started as a typical day for Wesley Autrey, a 50-year-old construction worker in New York City. It was about 12:45 P.M., and he was waiting on a subway platform to take his daughters home before he went to work. He suddenly noticed a man nearby have convulsions and collapse. Mr. Autrey and two women went to help the stranger. The man, Cameron Hollopeter, managed to get to his feet, but then stumbled at the edge of the platform and fell onto the subway tracks. Mr. Autrey looked up and saw the lights of the subway train approaching through the tunnel.

What would you do? Stand horrified and watch helplessly? Most people would jump in to help, but only if there were no train in sight. Mr. Autrey acted quickly. He leapt down onto the track. He realized that he didn't have time to get Mr. Hollopeter and himself back up on the platform before the train arrived, so he lay on top of the man and pressed down as hard as he could. Although the driver tried to stop the train before it reached them, he couldn't. Five cars passed over them before the train finally stopped. The cars had passed only inches from his head. His first words were to ask the onlookers to tell his daughters he was OK.

New York loves a hero. And there was no question that Mr. Autrey's actions had been just that – heroic. He became an overnight sensation. People couldn't get enough of the story. The media named him the "Subway Superman." New York City Mayor Michael Bloomberg gave him the Bronze Medallion, the city's highest honor. (In the past, this

honor has gone to such people as General Douglas MacArthur, Martin Luther King Jr., and Muhammad Ali.) Mr. Autrey was also asked to appear on several high-profile television talk shows.

His selfless bravery was also rewarded with money and gifts. Among other things, Mr. Autrey received: $10,000 from Donald Trump, a $5,000 gift card from the Gap clothing store, a new Jeep, tickets and backstage passes to a Beyoncé concert, and a free one-year public transit pass. A "Disney ambassador" thanked him with a one-week all-expenses-paid trip to Disney World and tickets to see *The Lion King* on Broadway.

How did Autrey, a Navy veteran, react to all this? Honorably. He said, "I don't feel like I did anything spectacular; I just saw someone who needed help. I did what I felt was right."

B Read the article again. Are these statements true or false? Choose the correct answer. Correct the false statements.

	True	False
1. Autrey hadn't noticed Hollopeter before he fell onto the tracks.	☐	☐
2. There was very little space between Autrey and the bottom of the train.	☐	☐
3. Autrey jumped onto the tracks because he wanted to be a hero.	☐	☐

C Group work Discuss these questions.

1. Have you ever had the opportunity to help someone in trouble or in danger?
2. Why do you think so many businesses wanted to reward Mr. Autrey?

12 MOVING AROUND

LESSON A ▶ *Culture shock*

 STARTING POINT

The benefits of studying abroad

A Read this website. Choose three benefits of studying a language abroad that you feel are the most important.

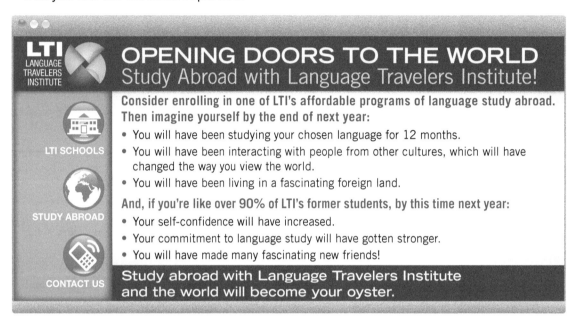

LTI
LANGUAGE
TRAVELERS
INSTITUTE

LTI SCHOOLS

STUDY ABROAD

CONTACT US

OPENING DOORS TO THE WORLD
Study Abroad with Language Travelers Institute!

Consider enrolling in one of LTI's affordable programs of language study abroad. Then imagine yourself by the end of next year:

- You will have been studying your chosen language for 12 months.
- You will have been interacting with people from other cultures, which will have changed the way you view the world.
- You will have been living in a fascinating foreign land.

And, if you're like over 90% of LTI's former students, by this time next year:

- Your self-confidence will have increased.
- Your commitment to language study will have gotten stronger.
- You will have made many fascinating new friends!

Study abroad with Language Travelers Institute and the world will become your oyster.

B Pair work Discuss your choices. What are some other benefits of studying or living abroad?

"I think interacting with people from other cultures is the most important benefit."

VOCABULARY & SPEAKING

Words of encouragement

A Complete these verbs and phrases with a preposition from the box.

about	in	of	to	with

1. adjust __*to*__
2. be excited _____
3. be scared _____
4. be familiar _____
5. become aware _____
6. get accustomed _____
7. look forward _____
8. participate _____
9. take advantage _____

B Pair work What challenges do people face when they live or study abroad? Discuss with a partner using the verbs and phrases in part A.

"Sometimes people are scared of starting a new job abroad because they aren't familiar with the routines."

VOCABULARY PLUS *see page 141*

3 GRAMMAR

Future perfect and future perfect continuous

Use the future perfect to emphasize that something will be completed or achieved by a particular point in the future.
By this time next year, your self-confidence **will have increased**.

Use the future perfect continuous to emphasize the duration of an activity in progress at a particular point in the future.
By the end of next year, you **will have been studying** your chosen language for 12 months.

GRAMMAR PLUS *see page 128*

A Look at the Starting Point on page 96 again. Can you find more examples of the future perfect and the future perfect continuous?

B These sentences about Joon's year abroad all have mistakes. Correct the mistakes using the future with *will*, the future perfect, or the future perfect continuous. Then compare answers with a partner.

1. By this time tomorrow, Joon ~~will travel~~ *will have been traveling* for 24 hours.

2. By the end of next week, he will have been receiving his student ID card and registered for classes.

3. He'll be going out more after a few weeks because he will have been more familiar with the city.

4. After studying English for a few months, he will have felt more confident about speaking to people.

5. By this time next year, his younger sister will have been visiting him once or twice. When she's older, she probably will have wanted to study abroad, too.

6. I'm sure he will change a lot by the time he comes back to Korea.

7. His family will have been surprised when he gets back because he will have been changing so much.

8. And just think – the next time we see him, Joon will turn 22 already, and he will be away for a year!

C Use these time expressions to write sentences using the future perfect or future perfect continuous. Then share them with a partner.

1. Before this class ends, . . .
2. By the end of the day, . . .
3. By the end of the week, . . .
4. At the end of the year, . . .
5. In two years' time, . . .
6. By the year 2030, . . .

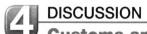

DISCUSSION
Customs and traditions

A Read this list of Canadian customs. Are they the same as or different from those where you live? Choose the correct answer.

	Same	Different
01 Both men and women shake hands with each other when they meet.	☐	☐
02 Business meetings are friendly, but there isn't much socializing beforehand.	☐	☐
03 Lunch is usually a fairly light meal that doesn't last long.	☐	☐
04 People are usually punctual for business appointments.	☐	☐
05 It's common to ask people you meet what kind of work they do.	☐	☐
06 Many people eat dinner early in the evening, around 6:00 P.M.	☐	☐
07 At the dinner table, the fork is generally held in the left hand and the knife in the right.	☐	☐
08 People offer to take their shoes off when entering somebody's home.	☐	☐
09 When invited to someone's home, a gift, such as flowers or dessert, is usually expected.	☐	☐
10 Most people open gifts as soon as they receive them.	☐	☐

B **Group work** How do you feel about the customs in part A? Explain your opinions.

"I think women should kiss on the cheek when they meet. Just shaking hands seems kind of cold somehow."

LISTENING
When in Rome . . .

🔊 **A** Listen to Andrew, Rachel, and Layla talking about their experiences abroad. Answer the questions.

1. What helped each of them get used to their new living situation?
2. What did each person find difficult to adjust to?

🔊 **B** Listen again. Did Andrew (*A*), Rachel (*R*), or Layla (*L*) do these things? Write the correct letter.

____ 1. felt homesick

____ 2. had fun playing a sport

____ 3. enjoyed food with friends

____ 4. didn't feel connected to others at first

____ 5. ate dinner late at night

____ 6. thought people talked about themselves too much

____ 7. enjoyed the old buildings

____ 8. watched comedy shows on TV

____ 9. tried to talk about herself

6 WRITING
Conclusions

The conclusion can close your composition by restating the main idea, summarizing the main points, looking to the future, making recommendations, or a combination of these methods.

A Read these two concluding paragraphs. Which methods do the writers use? Underline the parts of the conclusions that helped you decide.

Overall, for the majority of young people, taking a year off to travel has not replaced the traditional postsecondary pursuit of higher education. For most high school graduates, studying or training for a career will remain the most likely path. However, there are still many young people who save as much money as they can in order to see foreign sights and experience foreign cultures. Taking time to travel may put them behind a year as far as college and careers are concerned, but they say the personal growth is worth it.

In brief, there are real benefits to studying abroad. While it is certainly possible to learn the language in a country where it is not widely spoken, living abroad offers limitless possibilities for improvement. Additionally, foreign students have a real opportunity to hone their life skills. Generally, they are responsible for everything from money management, accommodations, and meals to ensuring that they have a good balance between their social life and school life. Studying abroad offers not only language lessons, but also life lessons, and is well worth considering.

B Find these linking words or phrases in the conclusions. How are they used? Do you know any others that have similar meanings?

   additionally   generally   however   in brief   overall

C Write a composition about living or traveling abroad. Choose one of these topics or one of your own. Your conclusion should use at least one of the methods described and some linking words or phrases.

   • culture shock   • group travel   • independent travel   • studying abroad

D **Pair work** Exchange papers with a partner and answer these questions.

   1. What methods did your partner use in his or her conclusion?
   2. Are the linking words used effectively? Why or why not?
   3. Can you offer any suggestions to improve your partner's conclusion?

1 STARTING POINT
Travel tips

A Read these people's experiences and the expert's advice. Can you think of any other advice?

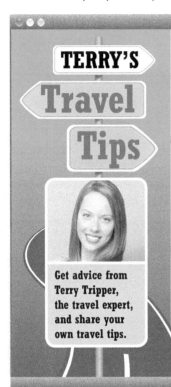

TERRY'S
Travel
Tips

Get advice from
Terry Tripper,
the travel expert,
and share your
own travel tips.

Meg B. says: *A woman fell down in front of me during a sightseeing tour. I helped her up, but soon after, I couldn't find my wallet. Do you think she might have taken it?*

Terry says: **It's very likely. If you hadn't been so nice, you would probably still have your wallet. It's a common scam – someone pretends to be in trouble, but actually turns out to be a thief!**

Bruno H. says: *I want to share a tip my friend gave me that I used on my last vacation. If you're worried about losing your passport, like I am, don't carry it around with you. Just keep it in your hotel room.*

Terry says: **That is a good tip if there is a safe in your room. If not, keep your passport with you at all times. If someone had broken into your room, you would probably still be trying to get home!**

Kim N. says: *On my last trip abroad, I brought a little notebook and pen to help me communicate while shopping. If I couldn't find something, I'd draw a picture. If I hadn't had that notebook and pen, my friends wouldn't be thanking me for the awesome souvenirs I brought them!*

Terry says: **That's a great idea! When phrasebooks and dictionaries don't help, a picture can be worth a thousand words. But you know there are also some great apps for that, right? Check out this** <u>website</u>.

B Pair work What travel questions would you ask Terry? Tell your partner. Then try to offer advice to each other.

"I want to buy souvenirs from the places I'm going to visit, but I also like to travel light. Should I store them at the airport or somewhere else?"

"The best thing would be to mail them home. If you don't mind waiting, use surface mail instead of airmail. It's cheaper."

2 LISTENING
Things went wrong.

🔊 **A** Listen to Cindy and Scott talking about their travel problems. What happened to each person?

🔊 **B** Listen again. Choose the statements you think are probably true. Compare your answers with a partner. Give reasons.

- ☐ 1. Cindy has a unique, easy-to-see name tag on her luggage.
- ☐ 2. Cindy travels frequently.
- ☐ 3. Scott likes peace and quiet when he travels.
- ☐ 4. Scott slept soundly all the way to Panama City.

3 GRAMMAR

Mixed conditionals

Use *had / hadn't* + past participle and *would / wouldn't* to talk about hypothetical events in the past that have effects on the present.

If you **hadn't been** so nice, you **would** probably still **have** your wallet!

If someone **had broken into** your room, you **would** probably still **be trying** to get home!

GRAMMAR PLUS *see page 129*

A Look at the Starting Point on page 100 again. Find another mixed conditional sentence. Does this sentence describe actual or hypothetical events?

B Complete these sentences with the correct form of the verbs in parentheses.

1. If I ____*had been*____ (be) more adventurous when I was younger,
   I ____*wouldn't have*____ (not have) any regrets about the things I missed.

2. The airline lost my luggage. If I _____ (bring) a change of clothes in my carry-on bag, I _____ (not shop) for new clothes now.

3. This flight is so long! If I _____ (not buy) an economy ticket,
   I _____ (be) more comfortable now.

4. If you _____ (learn) to speak some Mandarin before moving to Taipei, you _____ (be able to) ask someone for directions now.

5. If Martha _____ (not become) a flight attendant, she probably _____ (not travel) as much as she does.

4 DISCUSSION

Your own trip

A **Pair work** Have you ever had problems on vacation? Tell your partner. Use the topics below or your own ideas.

- health
- language
- accommodations
- getting around
- food
- costs
- safety
- weather

"I went to the beach last week, but the weather was awful."

"Why? Was it rainy?"

"No, it was too sunny. If it hadn't been so sunny, I wouldn't have this terrible sunburn now."

B **Group work** Share your bad travel experiences. Get advice about what you could have done differently.

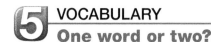

5 VOCABULARY
One word or two?

A Combine the items from the boxes to make compound adjectives.

culturally	assured	hearted	motivated
non	aware	judgmental	reliant
open	conforming	minded	sensitive
self			

culturally aware, nonjudgmental, open-minded, . . .

B **Pair work** Are the characteristics in part A important when you travel? Give an example for each one.

"If you're culturally aware, you'll find it easier to accept cultural differences."

VOCABULARY PLUS *see page 141*

6 ROLE PLAY
Planning a trip

A **Group work** Imagine you are planning a vacation. Discuss these questions. Write notes about what your group decides for each question.

1. Where would you like to go?
2. How long would you like your stay to last?
3. Would you like to go with a tour group or on your own?
4. What type of accommodations do you prefer?
5. What kinds of activities would you like to do during the day?
6. What sorts of evening activities would you prefer?
7. What would each person's budget be?
8. What types of transportation would you plan on using?

B **Class activity** Choose someone in your group to act as a travel agent and present your vacation to the class. The class votes on the best itinerary.

*"We have planned a truly exotic vacation for you in the remote Galápagos Islands!
You'll stay for seven unforgettable days in a five-star resort . . ."*

READING
Solo travel

A What are the best ways to experience a new place when you travel? Make a list. Then read the article to compare your list with the author's.

Get Yourself LOST

Travelers to a new city are often encouraged to take a bus tour. The thinking is that they can later return to the places that **captivated** them, but that's nonsense! What you see from the inside of a fast-moving bus is sanitized and unreal, utterly removed from the authentic sights, sounds, and smells outside.

The best way to experience any destination is by foot, without an itinerary, wandering where your spirit leads you. Even in the largest cities, the **savvy** traveler **plunges** into the very center of town and walks down the nearest street, experiencing the actual life of the people while looking into the grocery stores and courtyards. You eventually get to many of the same sites that are on the bus route – the museums, the monuments, the city hall – but you will have witnessed so much more because you will have felt the contemporary life of the city you're visiting.

"But what if I get lost?" people ask. No one ever gets permanently lost in a major city. Eventually, a trolley or bus passes with the words "Central Station" on its front and you can easily return to the center of town. Besides, the most wonderful things can happen if you do get lost, such as stopping at a sidewalk café to sit and relax and then asking directions from the locals at the next table. Hopefully, your trip may be **enhanced** by this encounter. Here are a few ways to make the most of your travels:

▶ **KNOW BEFORE YOU GO.** Before you depart, spend time learning about the history and

culture of your destination so you will better understand the place you're visiting.

▶ **MOVE AROUND LIKE A LOCAL.** Use the local subways, trams, and buses. You'll not only save money, you'll learn how people live there, and you'll gain a realistic perspective of the city.

▶ **CHECK THE BULLETIN BOARDS.** Bulletin boards list free lectures, concerts, workshops, and social gatherings, giving you a chance to join or meet the area's most **dynamic** residents.

▶ **TAKE A WALKING TOUR.** If you must book a guided tour, select the nonstandard, inexpensive kinds conducted on foot.

So, the next time you feel lured by a sightseeing bus tour, save your money and instead, wander around on your own. I promise you a time you'll remember fondly.

Source: "Get Yourself Lost," by Arthur Frommer

B Find the boldfaced words in the article. Then choose the correct words to complete the sentences.

1. If something **captivates** you, you're *upset / captured / delighted* by it.
2. A **savvy** traveler is *refined / experienced / adventurous*.
3. When you **plunge** into an activity, you probably *walk away from it / throw yourself into it / stumble into it*.
4. If you **enhance** your reading skills, you *upgrade / restore / prolong* them.
5. **Dynamic** people are more *cautious / unstable / interesting* than others.

C **Pair work** How do your travel habits compare with those in the article? Which ideas do you think you'll try the next time you visit a new city? Why?

COMMUNICATION REVIEW

UNITS 10–12

✔ SELF-ASSESSMENT

How well can you do these things? Choose the best answer.

I can . . .	Very well	OK	A little
▸ Describe annoying behavior (Ex. 1)	☐	☐	☐
▸ Make and respond to customer complaints (Ex. 1)	☐	☐	☐
▸ Discuss hypothetical situations in my present and future life (Ex. 2)	☐	☐	☐
▸ Understand the main points of a training workshop about customer service (Ex. 3)	☐	☐	☐
▸ Express and explain my opinions in a discussion about living and working in a different culture (Ex. 4)	☐	☐	☐
▸ Make hypotheses about past and present events in my life (Ex. 5)	☐	☐	☐

Now do the corresponding exercises. Was your assessment correct?

1 ROLE PLAY
Annoying customers

A What do you think annoys these people about their passengers or customers?

1. bus drivers
2. flight attendants
3. tech support workers
4. waiters/waitresses

"Something that probably makes bus drivers crazy is when people complain that the buses are running late. It usually isn't the drivers' fault."

B Pair work Take turns playing the role of a customer complaining and an employee responding to the complaints.

2 DISCUSSION
I'd like to try . . .

A Look at these questions and write answers that are true for you.

1. What is something you'd like to try, even if it were a little risky?
2. What is something you would do only if it were a matter of life or death?
3. Where is someplace you wouldn't want to go unless someone went with you?

B Pair work Discuss your answers with a partner.

"I'd like to try scuba diving at night, even if it were a little risky. I think diving in the ocean at night must be incredible."

LISTENING
Training

🔊 **A** Listen to a training workshop. What job are the trainees going to do?

🔊 **B** Listen again. Are these statements true or false? Choose the correct answer.

	True	False
1. Sammy would try to get the customer on a flight the same day.	☐	☐
2. Andrea says the customer should have left more time between flights.	☐	☐
3. Ricardo says the customer should be ashamed for being late.	☐	☐
4. Hannah would direct the customer to a place where she could get refreshed.	☐	☐

DISCUSSION
Culture shock

A Pair work How important are these personality traits for someone who is living and working in a new culture? Number them from 1 to 6 (1 = most important, 6 = least important).

It's important to be . . .

☐ culturally aware   ☐ nonjudgmental

☐ open-minded   ☐ self-assured

☐ self-aware   ☐ self-reliant

B Group work Join another pair. Explain your rankings to the group and discuss any differences of opinion.

DISCUSSION
What if . . . ?

A Pair work Discuss the questions.

How would your life be different today if . . .
1. you'd been born in another country?
2. you'd grown up in a much smaller or larger family?
3. you hadn't learned any English?
4. you hadn't met your best friend?

B Group work What event or circumstance has had the biggest effect on you? How would your life be different if that event hadn't happened?

"I think growing up in an extended family had the biggest effect on me. If my grandmother hadn't been living with us, I wouldn't have such an awareness of my culture and my ancestors."

GRAMMAR PLUS

7A Passive of present continuous, present perfect, future

If the agent (the person or thing doing the action) is unknown or obvious from the context, it's better to use a passive form. However, if the person or thing doing the action needs to be emphasized, it's better to use an active form.

The spyware **is being used** to collect information about college students. *(Agent is unknown.)*
Social networking sites **have been used** in criminal investigations. *(Agent is clear from context.)*
A criminal organization **has created** this virus, not an amateur hacker. *(Agent is emphasized.)*

The passive is very rarely used with the present perfect continuous. Use the passive of the present perfect instead.

People **have been posting** more videos to the Internet this year than ever before.
More videos **have been posted** to the Internet this year than ever before.

1 For each pair of sentences, is it better to use the passive or active form? Choose *a* or *b*.

1. ☑ a. More U.S. employers will likely allow access to social networking sites.
   ☐ b. Access to social networking sites will likely be allowed.

2. ☐ a. Soon, inventors will invent smartphones that don't require a battery.
   ☐ b. Smartphones that don't require a battery will be invented soon.

3. ☐ a. Most cell phone companies are now offering unlimited-use plans.
   ☐ b. Unlimited-use plans are being offered now.

4. ☐ a. Teachers might be teaching more high school students with educational computer games.
   ☐ b. More high school students might be taught with educational computer games.

2 Complete the sentences with the correct active or passive form of the verb in parentheses.

1. Recently, social networking sites *have become* (become) popular with all age groups.

2. Every week, free software _____ (download) on computers everywhere.

3. In the years to come, podcasts _____ (use) more often in educational programs.

4. Lately, children _____ (ask) for cell phones at a younger and younger age.

5. More sophisticated viruses _____ (create) all the time.

6. For years, hackers _____ (try) to use spyware to commit identity theft.

7. In years to come, more and more data _____ (store) in the cloud.

8. I recently discovered that my neighbors _____ (use) my Wi-Fi many times.

9. In the next decade, more job interviews _____ (hold) online.

10. Since I last visited this blog, several older posts _____ (remove).

7B Negative and tag questions for giving opinions

Use past negative and tag questions to offer an opinion about a past event and invite someone to react.
Wasn't it weird how the manager's microphone kept turning on and off during his speech?
Didn't it seem like the manager's speech would never end?
Shouldn't the company have provided us with coffee before the speech?
The manager's speech was really boring, **wasn't it**?
The manager has given some pretty boring speeches, **hasn't he**?
The manager's speech had just put about everyone to sleep when the fire alarm rang, **hadn't it**?

In informal spoken English, *they* can be used as the pronoun in tag questions when the subject is *somebody, someone, everybody, everyone, nobody,* or *no one.*
Everyone we know had a cell phone in school, didn't **they**?   Yes, they did.
Somebody has hacked into your computer, haven't **they**?   Yes, they have. / No, they haven't.

Use an affirmative tag question when the subject is a negative, such as *nobody* or *nothing.*
Nobody left any voice mail messages, **did they**?   Yes, they did. / No, they didn't.

1 Turn the statements into negative questions.

1. It would have been great if telemarketers had never gotten my number.
   Wouldn't it have been great if telemarketers had never gotten my number?

2. It was awful how much paper we wasted on fliers that nobody read.

3. Jill should have kept her text messages much shorter.

4. It was weird how those pop-up ads made my computer freeze.

5. It seemed like we spent all day looking for an Internet café.

6. It would have been great if we could have paid less for our computer.

7. We should have spent less time playing video games as kids.

8. It was sad how Mark got really addicted to social networking sites.

2 Complete the sentences with tag questions.

1. There were several voice mail messages for me, _weren't there_?

2. There haven't been any new rules about using social media at work, _____?

3. Someone told him there was a problem with his phone, _____?

4. You gave your computer password to someone, _____?

5. There was nothing he could do with his obsolete computer, _____?

6. Nobody we know ever actually clicked on those banner ads, _____?

7. She had already complained about the telemarketers, _____?

8. You used to have a robot vacuum that constantly cleaned the house, _____?

Non-defining relative clauses with *be* can be reduced in the same way as defining relative clauses. Notice the use of commas.

Einstein, **who is thought to be one of the greatest minds of the twentieth century,** struggled in school.
Einstein, **thought to be one of the greatest minds of the twentieth century,** struggled in school.
Curtis James Jackson III, **who is better known as the singer 50 Cent,** used to be a boxer.
Curtis James Jackson III, **better known as the singer 50 Cent,** used to be a boxer.

1 Rewrite these sentences using reduced relative clauses.

1. The photographer who lives upstairs has won many awards for his creativity.
   The photographer living upstairs has won many awards for his creativity.

2. Professional cooking, which is considered a tough business, requires both patience and skill.

3. Movie stars who are constantly hounded by the press deserve more privacy.

4. Roger Federer, who is ranked among the world's best tennis players, is considered very disciplined.

5. The Summer Olympics, which are held every four years, are broadcast around the world.

6. Children who are talented at music should take private lessons if possible.

2 Combine the sentences. Rewrite them as one sentence containing a reduced non-defining relative clause.

1. Lady Gaga is generally believed to be very confident and professional. She claims she is actually shy.
   Lady Gaga, generally believed to be very confident and professional, claims she is actually shy.

2. Yohji Yamamoto is famous for his modern fashion designs. He often uses the color black.

3. Jessica Alba has been interested in acting since the age of five. She first appeared in a film at age 13.

4. The movie *Twilight* was adapted from a novel by Stephenie Meyer. It stars Robert Pattinson.

5. Mark Zuckerberg is celebrated for creating Facebook. He attended Harvard University.

6. Justin Bieber is originally from Canada. He began his professional singing career in the U.S.

7. Tim Berners-Lee is credited with inventing the Web. He published the first website in 1991.

8. Jamie Oliver is known for his food-focused TV shows. He advocates healthier food in schools.

8B Non-defining relative clauses as sentence modifiers

Non-defining relative clauses can be used as sentence modifiers and can contain almost any verb. Some of the most common ones are *surprise, depress, encourage, suggest (that), contribute to*, and *result in*. Note that the verbs that describe emotion must be followed by an object.

My husband tried to repair a leak with aluminum foil, **which has resulted in a ruined silk carpet**.

My teacher praised my English today, **which encourages me to study harder**.

Peter has been happier since he took up golf, **which suggests that hobbies are good for a person both mentally and physically**.

I learned how to clean jewelry with toothpaste, **which depressed me because it meant I had wasted a fortune on expensive cleaners**.

I've started making my own clothes, **which has contributed to financial savings and a full closet**!

1 Match these statements with the appropriate non-defining clauses.

1. I use dental floss to string beads for jewelry, _c_

2. My sister always loved school, ____

3. Robert moved to a small town, ____

4. I just had a big fight with Ana, ____

5. Paul is really good at solving problems, ____

6. Amy jogs every morning, ____

7. I've had a private tutor for the past few months, ____

8. The class I wanted to take is already full, ____

a. which surprised us since he loves cities.

b. which has contributed to weight loss and more energy.

c. which is why I have so much of it.

d. which is why people always go to him for help.

e. which has resulted in better grades for me.

f. which encouraged her to go into teaching.

g. which means I'll have to explore alternatives in the course schedule.

h. which depressed me because she's my best friend.

2 Complete the sentences with a phrase from the box.

which resulted in   which suggested   which depressed
which encouraged   which means   which surprised

1. I'm working late tonight, _____*which means*_____ I'll take a later train home.

2. My friend was in a local play, _____ me to try acting.

3. Our team lost the championship, _____ me and my friends.

4. Prices went down last year, _____ savings for many people.

5. Ted sent me a nice birthday card, _____ me since he usually doesn't do anything special for people's birthdays.

6. Dinner tasted terrible, _____ that I didn't follow the recipe correctly.

The following are additional common phrases that show contrast and exception.

Use *whereas*, especially in formal writing, to present contrasting information.
Whereas the bottled water market is huge in Italy, it is very small in Japan.

Use *except (for)* or *with the exception of* to show an exception within a group.
Everyone in my family, **except for** my mother, plays a musical instrument.
Everyone in my family, **with the exception of** my mother, plays a musical instrument.

1 Circle the correct answer to complete the sentence.

1. (*While*)/ *Unlike* Leo prefers a big breakfast, I just have coffee.

2. No one in the class, *except that / with the exception of* Eva, can speak German.

3. *In contrast to / While* city people, those who live on farms must have a car.

4. *Unlike / Except for* Thai women, Spanish women greet each other with a kiss.

5. I'm a typical Canadian, *whereas / except for the fact that* I don't like hockey.

6. Most Americans have dinner by 7:00, *whereas / unlike* in Spain people eat later.

7. Everyone on our street, *except that / except for* my family, has a pet.

8. *Unlike / While* me, all my friends are addicted to reality shows on TV.

2 Read about Alonzo and Jun. Complete the sentences with an expression to show contrast or exception. More than one answer is possible.

Alonzo (26 years old) . . .	Jun (21 years old) . . .
finished college four years ago.	is in his third year of college.
considers himself to be pretty typical.	doesn't think he's really typical.
plays and watches all kinds of sports.	doesn't play any sports.
isn't crazy about baseball.	doesn't watch any sport but baseball.
has a high salary and eats out often.	doesn't work and always cooks at home.
wears a suit on weekdays.	always dresses very casually.

1. Jun is still in college, *whereas / while* Alonzo has already graduated.

2. Alonzo considers himself to be pretty typical, _____ Jun doesn't.

3. _____ Jun, Alonzo is a big sports fan.

4. Alonzo is a fan of most sports _____ baseball.

5. Alonzo has dinner in restaurants, _____ Jun usually can't afford to eat out.

6. _____ Alonzo, Jun hardly ever dresses up.

7. Alonzo has a good job, _____ Jun isn't working now.

8. Jun and Alonzo are very different, _____ they are both in their 20s.

9B Past habitual with *used to* and *would*

To ask questions about a habitual action or situation in the past, use *Did . . . use to . . . ?*
(NOT *Would . . . ?*).
Did you use to listen to rock music when you were younger?
Did you use to share a bedroom with your little brother?

Use the negative question *Didn't . . . use to . . . ?* to confirm a guess about habitual actions
or a situation in the past.
Didn't you use to work at a grocery store after school?
Didn't he use to play on the school soccer team?

1 Write the questions to these responses. Use *Did . . . use to* or *Didn't . . . use to*.

1. A: *Did / Didn't you use to live in San Francisco?*
   B: Yes, I did. I lived in San Francisco for about two years.

2. A: _____
   B: A lot? No, as a matter of fact, I've never drunk coffee.

3. A: _____
   B: No, he never did. Actually, Pete's allergic to cats.

4. A: _____
   B: In the school band? Yes, I did. I played the flute.

5. A: _____
   B: Yes, I always rode my bike in elementary school, but I'd take the bus on rainy days.

6. A: _____
   B: Yeah, my hair was really long, but I had to cut it when I joined the swim team.

2 Choose the correct answer to complete each sentence. Sometimes both are possible.

1. Lesley *would / used to* live in Brazil before she moved to Turkey.

2. We *would / used to* have fun during summer vacations.

3. They *would / used to* have a house by the ocean, but they've sold it.

4. Serena *would / used to* go mountain biking every weekend.

5. *Would her parents / Did her parents use to* own a Mexican restaurant ten years ago?

6. My mother *would / used to* volunteer at the hospital every winter.

7. Alex *would / used to* like to build models of cars and ships.

8. *Would you / Did you use to* be good at fixing cars when you were younger?

In some relative clauses, the relative pronoun (*who*, *that*, or *which*) can be omitted.

In an object relative clause, a relative pronoun (*who*, *that*, or *which*) is optional. Relative pronouns are only required when they function as the subject of a relative clause.
My friend told our classmates a secret. I had told him that secret.
My friend told our classmates a secret (**that**) I had told him.

In a subject relative clause, a relative pronoun (*who*, *that*, or *which*) is necessary because it functions as the subject of the relative clause.
I have a roommate. She never cleans the kitchen.
I have a roommate **who** never cleans the kitchen.

1 Choose the sentences where the relative pronoun (*who*, *that*, or *which*) is optional.

☑ 1. The restaurant that we had dinner at last night overcharged us.

☐ 2. One thing that makes me sick is really selfish people.

☐ 3. People who chew gum loudly really get on my nerves.

☐ 4. Someone's cell phone kept ringing all through the movie that I saw last night.

☐ 5. I had a big argument with a store clerk who refused to give me a refund.

☐ 6. My teacher gets mad at every little noise that our class makes.

☐ 7. The town fined a neighbor who burned garbage in her backyard.

☐ 8. The people in the line which he tried to cut into complained to the theater manager.

2 Complete the sentences with *who* or *that*. If the pronoun can be omitted, write *X*. Sometimes more than one answer is possible.

1. One thing _____*that*_____ gets me down is people ___*who / that*___ lie to me.

2. I like people _____ stand up for something _____ they believe in.

3. Something _____ makes me sad is people _____ have no place to live.

4. Something _____ I can't do is keep up with technology.

5. I was a kid _____ had parents _____ made a lot of rules.

6. The thing _____ aggravates me most is people _____ are cruel to animals.

10B Simple and complex indirect questions

If the beginning clause of an indirect question is in statement word order, the sentence is a statement and ends with a period.

I'm curious about why he didn't complain to the landlord.

I'm not sure who is responsible for repairing the roads.

The big question is if / whether we can get the city officials to listen to our concerns.

If the beginning clause of an indirect question is in question word order, the sentence is a question and ends with a question mark.

Do you have any idea if / whether I need a visa to visit China?

Could you tell me where I can go to pay my parking ticket?

Don't you wonder how a place with such poor service stays in business?

1 Rewrite these sentences using the words in parentheses.

1. Why can't the city add more streetlights? (I don't understand . . .)
   I don't understand why the city can't add more streetlights.

2. Is the city going to improve the rush hour bus service? (Do you know . . .)

3. Why are prices going up so fast? (. . . is something that baffles me.)

4. How can I finish the work before the deadline? (I have no idea . . .)

5. Have you saved enough money for school? (Would you mind telling me . . .)

6. Why aren't there any bike paths in the city? (. . . is beyond me.)

7. How am I going to find time to enjoy myself? (My main problem is . . .)

8. When are they going to build a new hospital? (Do you have any idea . . .)

9. Who decided to close the swimming pool in the park? (Don't you wonder . . .)

10. Is tuition going up again next year? (I have to find out . . .)

2 Rewrite these sentences as direct questions.

1. I haven't got a clue what we're supposed to do for homework tonight.
   What are we supposed to do for homework tonight?

2. How people can leave their children home alone is mystifying to me.

3. What I don't get is how I can keep up with all this new technology.

4. Why there isn't a pedestrian zone downtown is my number-one question.

5. I'd like to know who should be responsible for keeping our city clean.

6. Tell me what I have to do to get my driver's license.

7. When the next meeting will be is something I haven't found out yet.

8. I wonder if I should complain about my neighbor's loud parties.

To ask a follow-up question after a yes/no question, a shortened conditional can be used, especially in spoken or informal English. The positive shortened conditional is *if so*, and the negative shortened conditional is *if not*.

Would you consider lying to a good friend to avoid hurting your friend's feelings? **If so**, what kinds of things would you lie about?

Are you sure your friends are loyal and trusting? **If not**, you shouldn't tell them your secrets.

1 Match the yes/no questions on the left with the follow-up questions on the right.

1. Would you say anything if a colleague called you by the wrong name? __c__

2. If the man next to you on the bus fell asleep on your shoulder, would you wake him up? ____

3. Would you remain silent if you disagreed with your boss in a meeting? ____

4. Would you report it if you saw a friend steal a small item from a store? ____

5. If people you secretly disliked invited you to a party at their home, would you go? ____

6. If a cat always came to your house for food, would you keep it? ____

a. If not, what would you say?

b. If not, would you confront your friend?

c. If so, what would you say?

d. If not, would you try to find its owner?

e. If so, how would you wake him up?

f. If not, what excuse would you give?

2 Review the rules for the present unreal conditional with *unless*, *only if*, and *even if* on page 89. Choose the correct answer to complete each sentence.

1. I wouldn't lie to a friend (*unless*)/ *only if* it was in his or her best interests.

2. If you found money on the street, would you turn it in to the police? *If so / If not*, what would you do with it?

3. Would you report a shoplifter *only if / even if* the person looked poor? *If so / If not*, would you tell the store manager, or would you call the police?

4. He wouldn't lose his temper *only if / even if* he were really angry.

5. Would you confront a friend who gossiped about you behind your back? *If so / If not*, what would you say?

6. I wouldn't read anyone else's mail *even if / only if* I were really curious.

7. Would you make a promise if you already knew you couldn't keep it? *If so / If not*, what would you do later when you didn't keep the promise?

8. I would criticize my friends *unless / only if* I knew a way to help them Improve.

11B Wishes and regrets

Wishes and regrets often use comparative words, such as *(not) enough*, *more*, *less*, and *better*, and intensifiers, such as *really* and *very*.

I did**n't** save **enough** money last summer.
I wish I had saved **more** money last summer.

I spent **too much** money on video games last year.
If only I had spent **less** money on video games last year.

I bought **too many** clothes this weekend.
I wish I had bought **fewer** clothes this weekend.

I do**n't** understand math very **well**.
I wish I understood math **better**.

I got **really** angry at my friend last night.
If only I had**n't** gotten **so** angry at my friend last night.

1 Complete the wishes and regrets with a word from the box.

better   fewer   harder   less   more   so

1. I don't have enough time to do volunteer work.
   I wish I had _____*more*_____ time to do volunteer work.

2. I don't know how to swim very well.
   I wish I knew how to swim _____.

3. I drank too much coffee before bed last night.
   If only I had drunk _____ coffee before bed last night.

4. The teacher thought the questions on the exam were much too easy.
   The teacher wished the questions on the exam had been _____.

5. Our class has too many assignments this week.
   I wish our class had _____ assignments this week.

6. I felt really sleepy in class and couldn't pay any attention.
   I wish I hadn't felt _____ sleepy in class and had paid attention.

2 Rewrite these sentences using the words in parentheses.

1. I wasn't very obedient in elementary school. (I wish . . .)
   I wish I had been more obedient in elementary school.

2. I refused to take piano lessons when I was young. (If only . . .)

3. I fell asleep at the computer last night, and now my essay is late. (I wish . . . Then . . .)

4. I exercised too much yesterday, so now I feel really tired. (If only . . . Then . . .)

5. Bob is shy and doesn't make friends easily. (Bob wishes . . .)

6. I'm not a very good cook. (If only . . .)

12A Future perfect and future perfect continuous

When using the future perfect or future perfect continuous, the particular point in the future
is often referred to in another part of the sentence.
By this time next year, your commitment to language study is going to have gotten stronger.
On August 1, I will have been living overseas for six months.
After a few months, you're going to have made real progress with English.
Before next spring, he will have finished most of his course work.
By the time you arrive in New York, Marisa will have already received the package you sent.
When the van arrives, I will have been packing for two days, and I probably won't have finished.
Before I leave for Paris, I will already have sold my house and put my things in storage.
After I finish this, I will have completed everything on my "to do" list.

1 Underline the words in each sentence that refer to a point in the future.

1. <u>By the spring</u>, Nate will have visited over a dozen different countries.

2. When the end of the week arrives, I will have written four exams.

3. Before long, I'll have been working on this puzzle for an hour. It's impossible!

4. I can't believe he's still sleeping! At 11:00, he'll have been sleeping for 12 hours.

5. When she leaves the house, she'll have had six cups of coffee.

6. If it continues, on Tuesday it will have been raining for three weeks.

7. After I stop working, I will have painted three of the rooms in my house.

8. By the time the plane lands, we will have been in the air for seven hours.

2 Complete the sentences with the future perfect or the future perfect continuous
form of the verb in parentheses.

1. By the end of class, I ___*will have learned*___ (learn) about the future perfect tense.

2. By the year 2030, I _____ (work) for several years.

3. Before she's 30, Sue _____ (make) her first million dollars.

4. At the end of his trip, Seth _____ (visit) four different countries.

5. After I finish this book, I _____ (read) all the titles you recommended.

6. By 11:00, how long _____ Dan _____ (watch) TV?

7. When I finish college, I _____ (be) in school for 16 years.

8. Pretty soon, I _____ (wait) for her for an hour. I'm getting annoyed!

9. We're late. By the time we get there, they _____ (finish) dinner.

10. On Friday of this week, Kara _____ (travel) for two months.

12B Mixed conditionals

Conditionals can appear in many forms. They can describe how situations in the past affect situations in the past, the present, or the future.

Use a past form in both the *if* clause and the result clause to talk about true events in the past.
When I was younger, if I **didn't behave** well, my parents **were** disappointed.
If we **got** lost during our trip last year, we just **asked** someone for directions.

Use the past perfect in the *if* clause and *would / wouldn't have* + the past participle of the verb in the result clause to talk about hypothetical situations in the past that had effects on the more recent past.
If I **had been born** with a good voice, I **would have started** my own band a long time ago.

Use the past perfect in the *if* clause and *would / wouldn't* + verb in the result clause to describe hypothetical situations in the past that have effects on the present.
If I **had studied** harder when I was in school, I **would have** a better job today.

Use the past perfect in the *if* clause and *would / wouldn't* + verb in the result clause to talk about hypothetical situations in the past that have effects on the future.
If she **had booked** her flight before now, she **would be** in Paris next week.
If I **hadn't taken** a year off from school, I **would be graduating** this June.

Complete these sentences with the correct form of the verbs in parentheses. Sometimes more than one answer is possible.

1. As a kid, I always _____*enjoyed*_____ (enjoy) school if I _____ (like) the teacher.

2. If I _____ (study) harder last year, I _____ (not have to) repeat the course this year.

3. If he _____ (not speak) Greek, his trip to Athens last year _____ (be) so enjoyable.

4. When I was young, if I _____ (see) a scary movie, I _____ (have) bad dreams.

5. When I was a kid, if my father _____ (go away) on a business trip, he always _____ (call) at 8:00 to say "Good night" to us.

6. If I _____ (spend) less money when I was younger, I _____ (have) a nice little nest egg in a few years.

7. If I _____ (not have) a fight with my friend yesterday, I _____ (go) to the party tonight.

8. If she _____ (show) more interest since she was hired, she _____ (get) the next promotion.

9. If I _____ (not lose) my passport, I _____ (fly) to Lisbon tonight.

10. If she _____ (not start) figure skating when she was four, she _____ (not be) in the last Olympics.

VOCABULARY PLUS

 7A Technology buzzwords

Use four words from the box to correct the underlined mistakes in the sentences.

apps   the cloud   download   post   spyware   Wi-Fi

1. My aunt recently started to <u>text</u> her recipes online to share with others. _____

2. Kyle said that <u>a blog</u> was secretly recording my online activity. _____

3. Angela downloaded some <u>podcasts</u> to play games on her smartphone. _____

4. My apartment building has installed <u>a virus</u>, so I can use my laptop anywhere in the building to get on the Internet. _____

7A Expressions for connecting ideas formally

Choose the correct words to complete the text.

Does technology keep you up at night?

Technology has had a positive impact on our lives, for the most part. (1) *Similarly /* (*As a matter of fact*) */ Additionally*, it's hard to imagine how we could live without our computers, smartphones, and apps. These things have made our lives so easy! (2) *Therefore / Nevertheless / As a result*, some technology issues keep me up at night. (3) *Likewise / On the other hand / For example*, what can we do about spyware? As soon as we download software to get rid of it, someone creates a new way to spy on our computers. (4) *For instance / In fact / Furthermore*, there's spyware's nasty cousin, the virus, which can ruin anyone's day. It's a constant battle to overcome these issues, but we can take some common sense steps. Always remember to back up your documents. (5) *In fact / Additionally / As a result*, update your software whenever you get alerts from the manufacturers. Doing these things can help keep technology a positive part of daily life.

7B Words for forms of communication

Cross out the words that do <u>not</u> fit the meaning of the sentences.

A: We're planning an ad campaign to launch a new athletic shoe. In addition to some television ads that look like cool music videos, we'll use (1) *billboards / ~~voice mail~~ / bumper stickers.*

B: Are you also considering (2) *banner ads / pop-up ads / spam* to reach wider audiences?

A: Yes, they're on our list of possibilities. We're also wondering if we should hire a professional basketball player to appear on (3) *a crawl / a bus wrap / an infomercial.*

B: That's a great idea. Now, you may want to know that our research showed that younger audiences think print ads are old-fashioned. They want everything to be digital, so don't use (4) *fliers / billboards / pop-up ads* anymore.

8A Qualities of creative people

Match the correct words to complete the sentences.

1. Nora has the _____f_____ to practice daily to achieve her dream of becoming an opera singer.

2. The director was _____ when he chose the actors for the cast. He chose quickly, and didn't ask anyone back for a second audition.

3. Ellie has been on several archeological digs in Asia and is _____ about ancient Chinese and Korean cultures.

4. Pablo is _____ to complete five paintings to enter in the art competition this spring.

5. Gino is _____ in his business; for example, he uses recycled materials to build homes.

6. Chad's science fiction stories are set 500 years in the future and show great _____.

a. decisive

b. resourceful

c. determined

d. knowledgeable

e. originality

f. discipline

8B Collocations for problem solving

Choose the correct words to complete the text.

Groupware

If you ever worked for a multinational company in the past, you know that sometimes it could take hours just to set up a meeting with your colleagues. To help improve productivity, technology companies explored various ways to (1) *find a mistake / find a solution* to the problem. They studied the way people worked and (2) *made a mistake / analyzed this information* to figure out how companies might work together more effectively and efficiently. Technological innovators (3) *explored the possibilities of / found problems for* using networked computers and digital office tools. Eventually, they were able to (4) *solve this problem / analyze the problem* by designing groupware, which is software that helps groups of people work together and share information on the Internet. With groupware, colleagues can set up a meeting quickly and have meetings via video, across several continents. And electronic file-sharing systems allow workers to (5) *find alternatives / organize information* and share documents instantly. Problem solved!

9A **Expressions related to accepting or changing things**

Choose the correct words to complete the conversation.

Amber: I just met your sister. She's so passionate about changing society! She really wants to (1) *follow the crowd* / *make waves* / *fit in*.

Becca: Oh yes, Olivia and I are pretty different. I tend to follow the rules and am much more (2) *conventional* / *rebellious* / *unconventional* than she is.

Amber: What was it like growing up in your family? Did your parents teach you to behave yourself and (3) *accept* / *stand up to* / *confront* society's rules?

Becca: Actually, our parents were pretty (4) *unconventional* / *amenable* / *conservative* in their attitudes. At a time when most of their friends were becoming bankers and lawyers, my parents helped set up food pantries to feed poor people in our town.

Amber: Well, that helps explain why Olivia is so active in organizing that free tutoring program at the community center. But why do you think you're so different from her?

Becca: I guess it's just my personality. I want to help people, but I'm kind of shy and don't like to (5) *fit in* / *follow the crowd* / *confront* people.

Amber: I think that's good! You're (6) *being your own person* / *being rebellious* / *making waves* after all.

9B **Expressions with *keep* and *stay***

Replace the underlined words in each sentence with an expression from the box above that means the same thing.

keep in touch   **keep out of trouble**   **keep things in perspective**   **stay awake**

1. Sofia is moving to a new neighborhood, but her friends hope she will <u>stay connected</u>.

   Sofia is moving to a new neighborhood, but her friends hope she will ___*keep in touch*___.

2. When Pedro gets stressed out about his challenging new job, he tries to <u>remember what's truly important in life</u>.

   When Pedro gets stressed out about his challenging new job, he tries to

   _____.

keep connected   **keep up with**   **stay awake**   **stay out of trouble**

3. Our economics class is difficult, and the professor assigns so many reports and research projects. How do you <u>get it all done</u>?

   How do you _____ it all?

4. Ever since Jack changed schools, he's been hanging out with the wrong crowd. I hope he can <u>avoid getting into a bad situation</u>.

   I hope he can _____.

10A Expressions with *drive*, *get*, and *make*

Cross out the words that do not fit the meaning of the sentences.

Hey, friends, I just returned from a wonderful trip to Bangkok! What amazing street life there! And the food was so spicy and delicious. But traveling there drove (1) *me crazy* / *me down* / *me mad*. My flight from Los Angeles was cancelled because of some bad storms. There were long lines to rebook flights, but what made (2) *my blood boil* / *me mad* / *on my nerves* was the airline's terrible customer service. It took an hour to get my ticket for a new flight, and then I had to wait two more hours to get through security. Standing in line always gets (3) *me sick* / *on my nerves* / *under my skin*. I got stuck behind a family with six noisy, spoiled kids. I was thinking to myself, "Excuse me, but I just used all of my savings for this ticket, and I have to board my flight in 10 minutes!" Talk about driving (4) *someone upset* / *someone up a wall* / *someone mad!*

When I finally got on the plane, I ended up sitting next to a guy who kept talking about his big, important job. He bragged so much that it made (5) *my blood boil* / *me down* / *me mad*. To get him to stop talking, I pretended to fall asleep. I was so happy when our flight landed!

10B -ed words that describe feelings

Use words from each box to correct the underlined mistakes in the sentences.

baffled   infuriated   insulted

1. Max read over the instructions in his new computer manual several times, but he was still <u>stunned</u>. The instructions were not written very clearly. _____ *baffled* _____

2. My boss is impatient and gets angry when she has to wait for things. She was <u>saddened</u> that she had to wait for six months to get a refund for a defective cell phone. _____

3. In some cultures, people feel <u>enraged</u> if new acquaintances refuse to shake hands. _____

frustrated   mystified   stunned

4. Julia was <u>confused</u> because her rent was due on the first of the month, but she wouldn't get her paycheck until the following week. _____

5. After the doctor disappeared, the detective conducted a thorough investigation. Even after analyzing all the evidence, he was still <u>demoralized</u> about what had actually happened. _____

6. Vicky didn't think her violin audition went very well, so she was <u>humiliated</u> to learn that the conductor had selected her for first chair in the orchestra. _____

11A

Choose the true statement for each sentence.

1. Nick thinks it's unethical to tell a white lie, even if it's to protect someone's feelings.
   ☑ a. Nick thinks it's dishonest to tell a white lie.
   ☐ b. Nick thinks it's irresponsible to tell a white lie.

2. Mai believes that making wishes is irrational, and that it gives people false hopes.
   ☐ a. Mai thinks that making wishes is disagreeable.
   ☐ b. Mai thinks that making wishes is illogical.

3. The accountant is scrupulous about tracking all of the company's profits.
   ☐ a. The accountant is agreeable.
   ☐ b. The accountant is responsible.

4. Most lawyers think the judge has a solid reputation for being trustworthy.
   ☐ a. The judge's behavior is ethical.
   ☐ b. The judge's behavior is unacceptable.

5. The investigator reported that the bank's lending practices may be unscrupulous.
   ☐ a. The bank's lending practices may be illegal.
   ☐ b. The bank's lending practices may be irrational.

6. It's unfair to copy test answers from another student.
   ☐ a. It's illogical to copy test answers from another student.
   ☐ b. It's unethical to copy test answers from another student.

11B Adjectives and nouns referring to personal values

Choose the correct words to complete the conversation.

Yoko: One quality I value in my friends is (1) *indifference / selfishness /* (compassion).

Omar: I agree! I also think it's important for friends to be (2) *honest / tender / generous* if they think I'm doing something wrong.

Yoko: It's helpful when my friends are truthful, but I also want them to be
(3) *selfish / sensitive / resilient.* I don't want them to hurt my feelings.

Omar: Yeah, I guess that's important. You know, I wish some of my friends
were better at keeping secrets! They need to show a little (4) *discretion / kindness / tolerance* when I share something personal.

Yoko: That's true! I expect my friends to have (5) *generosity / resilience / respect* for my privacy. I'm pretty open, but it's annoying when people ask too many questions.

Omar: Yeah, some people are too curious. But, I think overall, my friends are
(6) *kind and generous / sensitive and selfish / resilient and indifferent,*
and they make me happy!

12A Expressions ending with prepositions

Choose the correct words to complete the email.

Hi Jill,

I heard that you're moving to Tokyo soon to teach English. That's something to (1) *be scared of /* ~~be excited about~~!

I remember that when I moved to Buenos Aires last year, it took a while to (2) *get accustomed to / look forward to* a new culture. I had to learn about the way people do business, make friends, and have fun. Luckily, I can speak Spanish, so I was able to (3) *be familiar with / participate in* meetings and conversations. I wanted to (4) *take advantage of / become aware of* cultural events, so I attended concerts, saw plays, and even learned to play guitar from an Argentinean musician!

My advice is to keep an open mind and give yourself time to (5) *adjust to / take advantage of* your new home. And don't (6) *be scared of / become aware of* trying new things.

I (7) *am familiar with / look forward to* hearing about your adventures in Japan!

Henry

12B Compound adjectives

Combine words from the boxes to make compound adjectives to complete the travel tips. Some words will be used more than once. Sometimes more than one answer is possible.

culturally   non   open   self

assured   aware   judgmental   minded   reliant   sensitive

Travel Tips

1. Be ___*open-minded*___ about trying new kinds of food. You may be captivated by a new cuisine!

2. Be _____ when it comes to exploring places on your own. You want people to think you're a confident, experienced traveler.

3. Be _____ when you experience new cultures. Consider all sides of an issue before forming an opinion.

4. People tolerate different levels of risk. Be _____ and assess your own tolerance for adventure, uncertainty, and possible danger when you plan your trips.

5. If you're traveling on business, learn about local customs and manners and try to be _____ when you meet with clients.

6. If you're going to hike in the mountains, prepare to be _____. Pack essentials such as water, food, rope, maps, a flashlight, and a first-aid kit.

Credits

Illustration credits

Charlene Chua: 8
Jo Goodberry: 20, 40, 60, 86
Brad Hamann: 72
Paul Hostetler: 5, 32, 33, 49, 51, 61, 78
Kim Johnson: 17, 43, 70, 80, 81

Larry Jost: 48
Dan McGeehan: 12, 55, 76, 93
Rob Schuster: 27, 28, 57
Koren Shadmi: 36, 88, 97, 133
James Yamasaki: 42, 82, 90, 104

Photography credits

Back cover: (*clockwise from top center*) ©Leszek Bogdewicz/Shutterstock, ©Wavebreak Media/Thinkstock, ©Blend Images/Alamy, ©limpido/Shutterstock; **2** ©iStock Collection/Thinkstock; **3** (*left to right*) ©iStock Collection/Thinkstock, ©Blend Images/Thinkstock, ©Stockbyte/Thinkstock, ©Digital Vision/Thinkstock; **4** (*top to bottom*) ©Purestock/SuperStock, ©iStock Collection/Thinkstock; **6** (*left to right*) ©Exactostock/SuperStock, ©yu liang wong/Alamy, ©Inmagine/Alamy; **7** ©Monkey Business/Thinkstock; **9** ©Stockbyte/Thinkstock; **10** (*left to right*) ©iStock Collection/Thinkstock, ©iStock Collection/Thinkstock, ©PhotoObjects/Thinkstock; **11** ©I love images/men's lifestyle/Alamy; **13** ©iStock Collection/Thinkstock; **14** (*top to bottom*) ©Gary Lee/Photoshot/Newscom, ©Courtesy of Banksy, ©Lia/Listal, ©Kathy deWitt/Alamy; **15** (*clockwise from top left*) ©Jupiterimages/Thinkstock, ©iStock Collection/Thinkstock, ©PHOTOPQR/L"ALSACE/Newscom; **16** ©NHPA/SuperStock; **18** (*clockwise from top left*) ©eye35.pix/Alamy, ©MIVA Stock/SuperStock, ©JTB PHOTO COMMUNICATI/JTB Photo/SuperStock, ©imagebroker.net/SuperStock; **19** ©Medioimages/Photodisc/Thinkstock; **21** (*top to bottom*) ©Neale Cousland/Shutterstock, ©iStock Collection/Thinkstock; **22** (*left to right*) ©John Foxx/Thinkstock, ©Brian Jannsen/Alamy; **24** (*clockwise from top left*) ©iStock Collection/Thinkstock, ©Jupiterimages/Thinkstock, ©Robert_s/Shutterstock; **25** (*top to bottom*) ©iStock Collection/Thinkstock, ©Hemis.fr/SuperStock; **26** ©Jupiterimages/Thinkstock; **27** (*top to bottom*) ©Blend Images/SuperStock, ©Prisma/SuperStock; **28** (*left to right*) ©Wavebreak Media/Thinkstock, ©iStock Collection/Thinkstock, ©iStock Collection/Thinkstock, ©Comstock/Thinkstock; **29** ©iStock Collection/Thinkstock; **30** ©Wavebreak Media/Thinkstock; **31** ©iStock Collection/Thinkstock; **35** ©iStock Collection/Thinkstock; **37** ©PhotoAlto/SuperStock; **38** (*left to right*) ©Tetra Images/SuperStock, ©Fancy Collection/SuperStock; **39** ©Ryouchin/Getty Images; **40** (*left to right*) ©Comstock/Thinkstock, ©Andrea Morini/Thinkstock, ©iStock Collection/Thinkstock; **44** ©Alain SHRODER/Getty Images; **45** ©iStock Collection/Thinkstock; **46** ©Ammit/Thinkstock; **47** ©Greg Wahl-Stephens/Associated Press; **50** ©Purestock/Thinkstock; **52** ©iStock Collection/Thinkstock; **53** ©Jupiterimages/Thinkstock; **54** ©iStock Collection/Thinkstock; **56** ©iStock Collection/Thinkstock; **58** (*clockwise from top left*) ©Jupiterimages/Thinkstock, ©Creates Images/Thinkstock, ©iStock Collection/Thinkstock, ©Blend Images/SuperStock; **62** (*left to right*) ©iStock Collection/Thinkstock, ©Karen Moskowitz/Getty Images, ©Mircea Bezergheanu/Shutterstock, ©Comstock/Thinkstock; **63** ©Zuma Press, Inc/Alamy; **65** ©iStock Collection/Thinkstock; **66** (*left to right*) ©Ablestock Collection/Thinkstock, ©iStock Collection/Thinkstock, ©You Touch Pix of EuToch/Shutterstock; **67** (*left to right*) ©iStock Collection/Thinkstock, ©Fuse Collection/Thinkstock, ©iStock Collection/Thinkstock; **68** (*left to right*) ©Bloomberg/Getty Images, ©Denise Kappa/Shutterstock; **69** ©Yoshikazu Tsuno/AFP/Getty Images/Newscom; **73** ©meshaphoto/Getty Images; **74** ©Kinga/Shutterstock; **75** (*left to right*) ©Glow Images/Getty Images, ©iStock Collection/Thinkstock, ©Image Source/Thinkstock; **77** (*left to right*) ©prudkov/Shutterstock, ©prudkov/Shutterstock; **79** ©Wavebreak Media/Thinkstock; **84** (*clockwise from top left*) ©Allison Joyce/Stringer/Getty Images, ©iStock Collection/Thinkstock, ©iStock Collection/Thinkstock, ©Stockbyte/Thinkstock, ©GoGo Images Corporations/Alamy, ©mikute/Shutterstock; **87** ©Andrew Vaughan/Associated Press; **91** ©Wavebreak Media/Thinkstock; **92** (*top to bottom*) ©iStock Collection/Thinkstock, ©Jupiterimages/Thinkstock, ©Hemera Collection/Thinkstock, ©Digital Vision/Thinkstock, ©Exactostock/SuperStock, ©iStock Collection/Thinkstock; **94** ©RubberBall/Alamy; **95** ©NY Daily News/Getty Images; **98** (*top to bottom*) ©Harry How/Staff/Getty Images, ©Robin Smith/Getty Images; **100** ©Design Pics/SuperStock; **101** (*left to right*) ©Belinda Images/SuperStock, ©frans lemmens/Alamy, ©I love images/city break/Alamy; **102** (*left to right*) ©iStock Collection/Thinkstock, ©Top Photo Group/Thinkstock, ©iStock Collection/Thinkstock; **103** ©Morgan David de Lossy/Corbis; **130** ©AFP/Getty Images; **135** ©Aurora Photos/Alamy; **137** ©Cultura Creative/Alamy; **141** ©Michael Coyne/Getty Images

Text credits

The authors and publishers acknowledge the following sources of copyright material and are grateful for the permissions granted. While every effort has been made, it has not always been possible to identify the sources of all the material used, or to trace all copyright holders. If any omissions are brought to our notice, we will be happy to include the appropriate acknowledgments on reprinting.

9 Adapted from "My Tribe," by Erin Peterson, *Experience Life*, September 2005. Reproduced with permission of Erin Peterson; **17** Adapted from "Amnesia Spoils Newlyweds' Bliss," *ABC News*, June 30, 2005. Reproduced with permission of ABC News; **43** Adapted from "What Type of Cell Phone User Are You?" by Nancy Friedman. Reprinted with permission of Telephone Doctor Customer Service Training in St. Louis, MO. Nancy Friedman, President, is a keynote speaker at association meetings and Chamber of Commerce events as well as corporate gatherings. Call 314.291.1012 for more information or visit the website at www.telephonedoctor.com; **61** Adapted from "Brother, can you spare a dimo for my Gucci bills?" by Janelle Brown, *Salon*, October 2, 2002. This article first appeared in Salon.com, at www.salon.com. An online version remains in the Salon archives. Reprinted with permission; **69** Adapted from "Mr. Song and Dance Man," by Dr. David McNeill, *Japan Focus*. Reproduced with permission of Dr. David McNeill, Sophia University, Tokyo; **77** Adapted from "4 Ways to Brush Up Your Problem-Solving Skills," by Barbara T. Armstrong, October 24, 2012. Reproduced with permission of Barbara T. Armstrong, Kahler Slater, Inc.; **87** Adapted from "Dave Carroll is still having problems with airlines," by Ellen Roseman, *The Toronto Star*, May 18, 2012. Reprinted with permission of Torstar Syndication Services; **103** Adapted from "Get Yourself Lost," by Arthur Frommer, *Travel Holiday*, September 1994.

Answers

Page 44, Exercise 1B: Story 3 is false.

Jack C. Richards & Chuck Sandy

Passages

Third Edition

Video Activity Worksheets

1B

CAMBRIDGE
UNIVERSITY PRESS

7 UNAPPRECIATED TECHNOLOGIES

Before you watch

A Match the inventions with the pictures. Then check answers with a partner.

a. refrigerator   c. plumbing   e. barcode   g. credit card
b. zipper   d. shipping container   f. pocket calculator   h. ATM / cash machine

1. ____   2. ____   3. ____   4. ____

5. ____   6. ____   7. ____   8. ____

B **Pair work** When do you think people started using the inventions in part A? Complete the chart with the names of the inventions. Then compare answers with your partner.

Thousands of years ago	Early 1900s	1950s	1960s and 1970s	1990s

While you watch

A Select the summary that best describes this episode of *Tech Talk*. Then check your answers to *Before you watch* part B.

☐ 1. This episode of *Tech Talk* discusses household inventions that will make our lives easier in the future.

☐ 2. This episode of *Tech Talk* covers inventions that are so common that they aren't always listed as great inventions.

☐ 3. This episode of *Tech Talk* talks about the importance of inventions that people don't know that much about.

☐ 4. This episode of *Tech Talk* explains why email and the Internet were not thought to be important at first.

B Write *T* (true) or *F* (false). Then correct the false statements with a partner.

_____ 1. The inventions covered in this episode of *Tech Talk* are new.

_____ 2. Plumbing was not brought inside the home as soon as it was invented.

_____ 3. Because of shipping containers, products from abroad can be as affordable as local products.

_____ 4. Barcodes make things cheaper for stores because tracking, pricing, and selling are all done faster.

_____ 5. Both hosts of *Tech Talk* agree that the ATM is the most important invention in finance.

_____ 6. According to *Tech Talk*, the Internet is the best invention because it speeded up communication.

C Choose the item or action the video mentions as being improved or replaced by these inventions.

1. refrigerators
   a. shopping for food
   b. eating ice cream
   c. going to the store

2. zippers
   a. hooks and clasps
   b. buttons
   c. ties and laces

3. plumbing
   a. using bottled water
   b. going to a well
   c. carrying buckets

4. shipping containers
   a. loading and unloading boats
   b. cardboard boxes
   c. shipping by truck

5. barcodes
   a. finding products
   b. tracking products
   c. using money

6. pocket calculators
   a. doing homework
   b. doing taxes
   c. counting on your fingers

7. credit cards
   a. writing personal checks
   b. using cash
   c. carrying a handbag

8. ATMs
   a. bank clerks
   b. waiting in lines
   c. making deposits

9. email
   a. writing by hand
   b. time needed to communicate
   c. making phone calls

After you watch

A Think about what you learned from the video. Then answer the questions.

1. Which invention from *Tech Talk* do you think is the greatest? Why?

_____

_____

2. Which invention from *Tech Talk* do you think is the least important? Why?

_____

_____

3. Which invention from *Tech Talk* do you think is the most unappreciated by a majority of people? Why?

_____

_____

B **Pair work** Compare your answers from part A. Give reasons and examples to support your opinions.

C **Group work** Create a list of the top five most important inventions or technologies *not* mentioned in *Tech Talk*. Talk about how life has been changed or improved by each invention to support your choices.

Before you watch

A In your opinion, which are the most important traits an actor needs? Choose the top 10 traits from the list.

☐ adventurous   ☐ expressive   ☐ organized

☐ creative   ☐ good-looking   ☐ passionate

☐ curious   ☐ innovative   ☐ patient

☐ determined   ☐ lucky   ☐ physically fit

☐ enjoys attention   ☐ motivated   ☐ a strong voice

B **Pair work** Compare your answers. For each trait, discuss why or why not an actor would need that trait.

While you watch

A Choose the topics the actor mentions in the video.

☐   1.   when he first knew he wanted to be an actor

☐   2.   what working as a child actor is like

☐   3.   what the schedule of an actor is like

☐   4.   how to deal with the audition process

☐   5.   how to handle tough competition

☐   6.   the top school for acting training

☐   7.   which kinds of acting work pay better

☐   8.   his least favorite acting job

☐   9.   the best costume he ever wore

☐ 10.   his favorite acting job

☐ 11.   what is best about being an actor

☐ 12.   traits that an actor should have

☐ 13.   how long an actor's career usually is

☐ 14.   how many fans he has

B Complete the sentences with the correct words from the video.

1. "I needed an outlet . . . to have . . . to put out my _____ side."

2. "To become an actor, you have to have _____ for the work."

3. "You have to be really _____ to get yourself up . . . every day, to get out there every day, and . . . give it your all."

4. "To be an actor . . . you have to have a strong sense of _____ and a lot of _____."

5. "Someone who has a lot of _____ would be a good actor."

6. "Someone who has a really _____ would be a great actor."

7. "Someone who enjoys _____ would be a great actor."

C Choose the correct answers according to the information in the video.

1. The actor decided what he wanted to do for the rest of his life while performing
   _____.
   a. at an amusement park   b. for the Cub Scouts   c. at the Boston Common

2. The real work of acting is _____.
   a. dealing with auditions   b. performing in theaters   c. staying motivated

3. Because it pays more, _____ is a better way to support an acting career.
   a. theater work   b. film work   c. amusement park work

4. The actor really enjoyed a job where he _____.
   a. was a comedian in Boston   b. did a Shakespeare play   c. worked on a big film

5. Patience is required to be an actor because _____.
   a. it's a hard lifestyle   b. it takes a long time to develop job security   c. it takes a while before it is fun

6. The actor thinks he will always be an actor because he _____.
   a. feels he is determined and passionate   b. wants to show his family he can be successful   c. can't see himself doing anything else

After you watch

A **Pair work** Discuss the questions.

1. Which of the traits from *Before you watch* part A does the actor in the video seem to have? Support and explain your answers.
2. Could you or someone you know be an actor? Think about the traits mentioned in the video and discuss why you feel this way.

B Other types of jobs might require different skills and traits. List five traits and the kinds of jobs in which they would be an advantage.

	Trait	Possible jobs
1.		
2.		
3.		
4.		
5.		

C **Writing** Choose a job you listed in part B. Write a paragraph about the job and include at least three additional traits that would make someone good at it. Explain why each trait would be necessary for the job.

Before you watch

A Select the qualities you think most employers are looking for when interviewing people for jobs.

☐ adaptable   ☐ has a sense of humor   ☐ thinks outside the box

☐ emotional   ☐ persistent   ☐ ultracompetitive

☐ fits in with others   ☐ playful   ☐ unconventional

B **Pair work** Compare your answers. Do you agree on what qualities most employers are looking for? Why or why not? Discuss your opinions.

While you watch

A Write *M* for Monica, *D* for David, or *A* for Ashley.

Monica

David

Ashley

1. Who saw the box as a platform? ____
2. Who worked on the same idea for nearly the entire five minutes? ____
3. Who tried to melt wax to stick the candle to the wall? ____
4. Who was unable to think of additional approaches due to stress? ____
5. Who playfully tried a bunch of solutions? ____
6. Who tried several approaches but still didn't find a solution? ____

B Write the letter of the correct phrase to complete each sentence according to information in the video.

a. being able to preserve a sense of humor   d. looking for other perspectives
b. fitting in with the company   e. thinking outside the box
c. thinking about the problem in new ways   f. being persistent

1. Before implementing hiring tests, companies used to hire people based on ____ .
2. Except when trying the wrong idea, ____ is a good thing.
3. If people get overly frustrated, they will have difficulty ____ .
4. A good problem-solving strategy is ____ .
5. Studies show an important part of problem solving is ____ .
6. The person who solved the problem did it by ____ .

C Take notes to answer the questions in your own words. Then compare answers with a partner.

1. How did Mark Hernandez's company change how they measure candidates?

_____

_____

2. What does the problem of the matchbook, candle, thumbtacks, and corkboard reveal about each candidate?

Monica: _____

David: _____

Ashley: _____

3. What are the three main points that Mark mentions about problem solving?

_____

_____

_____

After you watch

A **Pair work** Given what you know about the candidates from how they tried to solve the problem, what kinds of jobs do you think each person would be good at? Why?

Monica: _____

_____

David: _____

_____

Ashley: _____

_____

B **Group work** Compare your answers from part A. Then work together to decide upon the best job for each candidate. Share your group's answers with the class. Be specific about the job and why it is the best fit for that person.

C **Writing** How can Monica and David improve their interviewing skills? Write some advice for them about how to better interview for the jobs you chose for part A. Support your ideas with facts, reasons, and examples.

Before you watch

A Label the pictures with the words in the box. Then check your answers with a partner.

ambulance	chalkboard	cicada	wind chimes
angle grinder	chainsaw	crows	vuvuzela horn

1. _____ 2. _____ 3. _____ 4. _____

5. _____ 6. _____ 7. _____ 8. _____

B Pair work Think about the sounds the items in part A make. Which do you think are loud or annoying? Which don't bother you at all? Discuss your opinions.

While you watch

A Cross out the items that you do *not* see or hear for each sound category in the video. More than one item may be crossed out for each.

1. Loud:

    an ambulance siren / drums / a train / a chainsaw

2. Annoying:

    wind chimes / crows / chalk on a board / glass breaking

3. Loud and annoying:

    rock music / cheering / vuvuzela horns / race cars

4. The most annoying:

    nails on a chalkboard / fire trucks / a knife on glass / angle grinders

5. Sounds people say annoy them:

    loud TVs / loud phone conversations / a family member's laugh /

    loud motorcycles / loud music / elevator music /

    cicadas / helicopters / a fork on glass

B Choose the statement that best summarizes the main idea presented at these points in the video.

1.

   a. News reporters often have problems with noise.

   b. People in cities often complain about noise.

   c. There are many loud and annoying sounds in the city.

2.

   a. The World Cup in 2010 was louder than usual.

   b. South African soccer players complained that the fans were too loud.

   c. The horns used by fans at the World Cup were particularly loud and annoying.

3.

   a. Some sounds are annoying but not that loud.

   b. Some types of sounds can actually hurt our hearing.

   c. Certain types of sounds bother the most people.

4.

   a. A baby's cry is one of the most stressful sounds to humans.

   b. Babies cry when they are annoyed by noise.

   c. People begin crying and screaming when stressed at an early age.

C Write the letter of the correct phrase to complete each sentence.

a. elevator music
b. the sound of an insect
c. people talking loudly on their cell phones
d. the sound of loud motorcycles
e. a certain person's laugh

1. Margaret Allen says she gets irritated by ____ .
2. Something that bugs James Williams is ____ .
3. Henry Snider and his son, Kyle, hate ____ .
4. Graciela Martinez feels sick from ____ .
5. Lisa Manap says what really gets under her skin is ____ .

After you watch

A Think about the sounds in the video. Make a list of the top five most annoying sounds for you. Give reasons for your choices. Then share your list with the class.

B **Pair work** Make a list of 10 other sounds, actions, or things that may be considered annoying. Rank them in order from *worst* (1) to *not so bad* (10).

C **Group work** Compare your lists from part B and make a final top 10 list of annoying sounds, actions, or things. Then share the list with the class.

11 THREE INTERNATIONAL STUDENTS DISCUSS AMERICAN VALUES

Before you watch

A Which of the following behaviors do you think are typical of people from the United States? Choose all that apply based on your opinion.

- ☐ tend to be on time
- ☐ tend to be late
- ☐ don't express emotion
- ☐ express emotion openly
- ☐ value freedom for the individual
- ☐ prefer to fit in with the group
- ☐ embrace rebelliousness
- ☐ respect the elderly
- ☐ are obedient to family
- ☐ believe people are equal
- ☐ think fate is predetermined
- ☐ believe people make their own fate

B **Pair work** Compare and discuss your answers for part A. Then select six behaviors you both agree are typical of Americans. Share your opinions with the class and give reasons to support your choices.

While you watch

A Choose the six topics discussed in the video.

- ☐ 1. friendships
- ☐ 2. time
- ☐ 3. food
- ☐ 4. emotions
- ☐ 5. individuality
- ☐ 6. families/groups
- ☐ 7. customs
- ☐ 8. equality
- ☐ 9. jobs
- ☐ 10. rewards from hard work

B Who says each sentence? Write *O* for Olivia, *H* for Hikaru, *R* for Ranbir, or *E* for Enku.

Olivia, the U.S. **Hikaru, Japan** **Ranbir, India** **Enku, Ethiopia**

____ 1. "Americans would think it disrespectful to be late unless they have a very good reason."

____ 2. "I often wish I could express my emotions with more freedom."

____ 3. "I wish I had a dollar for every time Americans talked about freedom!"

____ 4. "But then I realized: It's not about the freedom to do illegal things, but the freedom to be an individual."

____ 5. "It's more about the family than the individual."

____ 6. "But it's more about the group – fitting in with people at work, for example."

____ 7. "If we had been better about it from the beginning, I think we could have avoided a lot of war and violence."

____ 8. "I can't imagine not choosing the life I want to lead."

C Choose the correct answers according to the information in the video.

1. If you were in _____ , you might not worry about being late.

   a. Japan   b. the U.S.   c. Ethiopia

2. As an American, you might think of someone who is late as _____ .

   a. insensitive   b. respectful   c. important

3. In _____ , you would never yell at someone in public, even if you were very angry.

   a. Japan   b. India   c. Ethiopia

4. A young woman in _____ would do what her family wants.

   a. the U.S.   b. India   c. Ethiopia

5. Not everyone believes they can change their fate in _____ .

   a. Olivia's family   b. the U.S.   c. Ethiopia

6. A very uniquely American idea is that if you _____ .

   a. work hard, you can achieve whatever you want
        b. are born into a certain lot in life, you can't change it
        c. follow the path your parents choose, you will succeed

After you watch

A Make a list of the behaviors in *Before you watch* part A that are true about people in your culture.

B **Pair work** Compare your choices for part A and review the behaviors again. Which behaviors from part A do you agree are OK or normal in most cultures? Which are disrespectful in most cultures? Which depend on the culture a person is from? Complete the chart.

Acceptable	Disrespectful	Culturally dependent

C **Group work** Make lists of behaviors you think are generally acceptable or not acceptable in most cultures. Include at least three or four behaviors for each category. Present your lists to the class.

Generally acceptable	Generally not acceptable

12 AN L.A. GIRL IN BERLIN

Before you watch

A Imagine you are going to study in Germany for a year. Which five things would you have the most difficulty with? Number your choices from 1 (most difficult) to 5 (least difficult).

____ learning about a new city   ____ learning a new language   ____ different weather

____ getting around in a foreign country   ____ homesickness   ____ different food

____ taking classes in another language   ____ making friends   ____ different cultural ideas

B Pair work Compare your answers. How similar are your views? Discuss your choices and give reasons for your answers.

A: I think I'd have a difficult time eating different foods. I'm a picky eater.

B: Not me! I love to try new foods. I'll eat anything. But I can't stand being cold. I might have a hard time if the weather is cold.

While you watch

A Choose the statement that best summarizes the main idea presented at these points in the video.

1.
   a. Monica's classes are held in these old buildings.
   b. Monica has just arrived and she is excited.
   c. Monica feels Germany is very different from L.A.

2.
   a. Monica is excited to practice speaking with Germans.
   b. She enjoys relaxing with friends in her room every night.
   c. She has made new friends.

3.
   a. Monica cannot wait to go home for the winter holidays.
   b. She is enjoying her first cold weather and snow.
   c. Due to the weather, she finally had to figure out the trains.

4.
   a. Monica is sad to leave Berlin because she has met someone.
   b. She wants to stay another eight months.
   c. She likes the food and now feels more at home in Germany.

B Number the sentences from 1 to 7 in the order the topics are mentioned in the video.

____ Monica hopes that before she goes home, she'll have figured out the trains.

____ She is going to a holiday feast.

____ She thinks that before the year ends she will have become fluent.

____ She is surprised by how much she likes the food.

____ She is afraid that by the end of the year she will have only gotten to know her room.

____ She is beginning to feel connected to others, such as Julia and Annika.

____ She wouldn't have discovered her favorite spot in the city if she hadn't gotten lost.

C Take notes to answer the questions in your own words. Then compare answers with a partner.

1. Why is Monica scared in October?

   _____

   _____

2. What is the most difficult thing about December for her?

   _____

   _____

3. Why is April 16 an important day for Monica?

   _____

   _____

After you watch

A Pair work Discuss how Monica's attitude and experiences changed over the eight months she was abroad. What conclusions might one draw from this?

B Group work Compare your conclusions from part A with another pair. Discuss how they are the same or different.

C Writing Write a paragraph explaining how you feel about new and challenging experiences, such as studying abroad. Are these types of experiences fun, exciting, challenging, or frustrating for you? How do you handle these types of situations?

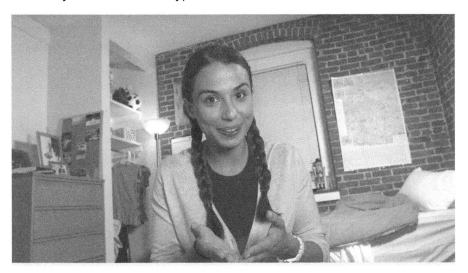

Video Activity Worksheets Credits

Video credits

Video screen grabs courtesy of Steadman Productions, Boston, MA: 200, 201, 206, 207, 208, 209, 211 (*top, center top*), 212, 213, 214, 215

Photography credits

192 (*left to right*) ©motion.pi/Shutterstock, Inc., ©Johan Larson/Shutterstock, Inc., ©Pressmaster/Shutterstock, Inc., ©Alexander Kirch/Shutterstock, Inc; **193** (*clockwise*) ©Johan Larson/Shutterstock Inc., ©motion.pi/Shutterstock Inc., ©Alexander Kirch/Shutterstock, Inc., ©Pressmaster/Shutterstock, Inc.; **194** (*top left to right*) ©Denis Dryashkin/Shutterstock, ©maggee/Shutterstock, ©Video supplied by Oxford Scientific/Getty Images; **195** ©wavebreakmedia/Shutterstock, Inc.; **196** (*top left to right*) ©Tidepool Stock/Shutterstock Inc., ©picture.uk/Shutterstock Inc., ©Gavin Hellier/Shutterstock Inc., ©OrlowskiDesigns/Shutterstock Inc., (*bottom left to right*) ©OrlowskiDesigns/Shutterstock Inc., ©dubassy/Shutterstock Inc., ©Holger Mette/Shutterstock Inc., ©Geoff Tompkinson/Getty Images; **197** (*left to right*) ©Hellier/Shutterstock Inc., ©Tidepool Stock/Shutterstock Inc., ©FootageFirm Inc., ©skyearth/Shutterstock Inc.; **198** (*top to bottom*) ©Neustock Media/Shutterstock Inc., ©footagefirst/Shutterstock Inc., ©wavebreakmedia/ Shutterstock, Inc., ©freeonestock/Shutterstock Inc.; **199** ©motion.pl/Shutterstock, Inc.; **203** (*center, bottom*) ©ReeldealHD/Shutterstock Inc., ©Dualstock/ Shutterstock, Inc.; **204** (*top left to right*) ©Wiktoria Pawlak/Shutterstock, ©Pixel Embargo/Shutterstock, ©Illin Sergey/Shutterstock, ©qingqing/Shutterstock; (*bottom left to right*) ©MJTH/Shutterstock, ©Todd Taulman/Shutterstock, ©cretolamna/Shutterstock, ©gualtiero boffi/Shutterstock; **210** (*top left to right*) ©Francois Arseneault/Shutterstock Inc., ©jim Barber/Shutterstock Inc., ©one_clear_vision/Shutterstock Inc., ©Dr. Michael Gellner/Shutterstock Inc., (*bottom left*) ©eFOOTAGE.com, (*bottom center left*) ©Sky News/Getty Images, (*bottom center right*) ©Alice Day/Shutterstock Inc.; (*bottom right*) ©Smit/Shutterstock Inc.; **211** (*bottom, center bottom*) ©Film Footage courtesy of Shutterstock Inc., ©Derek Thomas/Shutterstock, Inc.

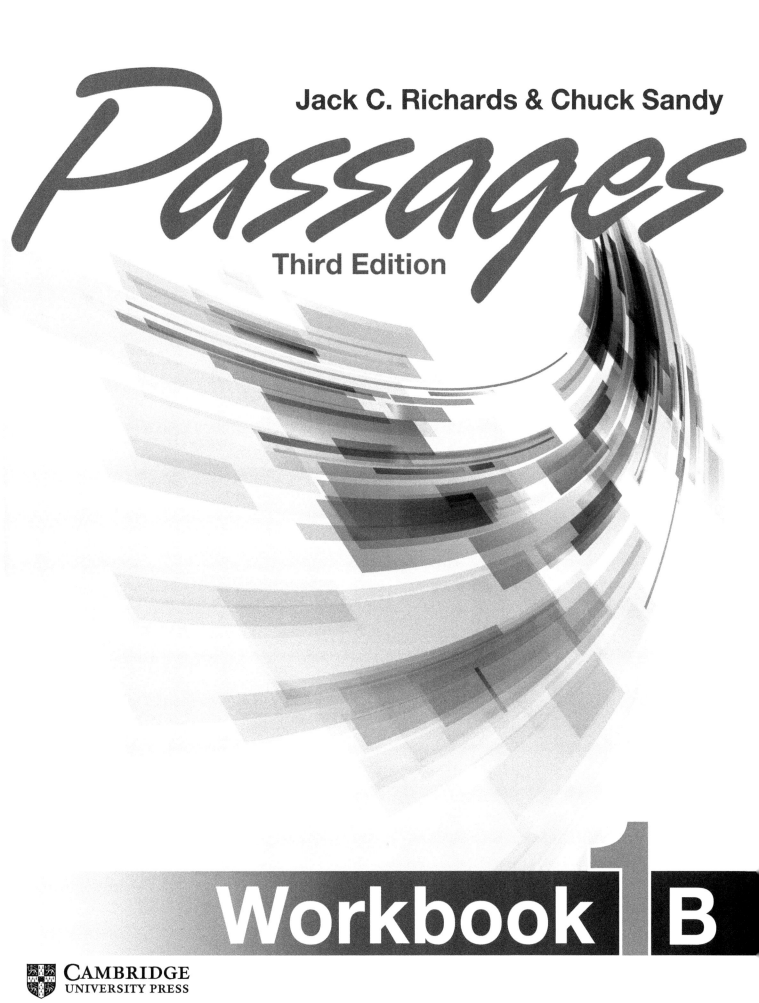

Jack C. Richards & Chuck Sandy

Passages

Third Edition

Workbook 1 B

CAMBRIDGE
UNIVERSITY PRESS

Contents

Credits

Illustration credits

Kim Johnson: 4, 28, 45, 66, 67
Dan McGeehan: 7, 54
Paul Hostetler: 8, 27, 56, 60, 64
Koren Shadmi: 33, 52, 62
James Yamasaki: 22, 35, 61

Photography credits

1 ©Chris Bennett/Aurora/Getty Images; **3** (*clockwise from top center*) ©Keith Levit/Design Pics/Corbis, ©iStock/Thinkstock, ©Iconica/Commercial Eye/Getty Images; **6** ©Barry Austin Photography/Getty Images; **9** ©iStock/Thinkstock; **10** ©dieKleinert/Alamy; **11** ©Holger Hollemann/dpa/picture-alliance/Newscom; **12** ©Christian Guy/Getty Images; **13** ©iStock/Thinkstock; **14** ©iStock/Thinkstock; **15** ©iStock/Thinkstock; **16** ©John W Banagan/Photographer's Choice/Getty Images; **18** (*top left to right*) ©trekandshoot/Shutterstock, ©iStock/Thinkstock, ©iStock.com/wdstock, ©A. T. Willett/Alamy; (*bottom*) ©Rudolf Balasko/Thinkstock; **20** ©Media Bakery; **23** ©Blue Jean Images/Alamy; **24** ©andresrimaging/iStockphoto; **26** ©Pulp Photography/The Image Bank/Getty Images; **29** ©iStock/Thinkstock; **30** ©Clover/SuperStock; **31** ©Eric Isselee/Shutterstock; **34** ©Elke Meitzel/age fotostock; **36** (*top to bottom*) ©assalave/iStockphoto, ©Antonio Balaguer soler/Thinkstock; **38** ©iStock/Thinkstock; **40** ©Wavebreak Media/Thinkstock; **41** ©iStock.com/DSGpro; **44** (*left to right*) ©Jodi/Jake/Media Bakery, ©Masterfile Royalty Free, ©Andresr/age fotostock; **46** ©Caspar Benson/fstop/Corbis; **47** (*left to right*) ©wavebreakmedia/Shutterstock, ©Juanmonino/E+/Getty Images, ©iStock.com/pressureUA, ©homydesign/Shutterstock; **48** (*top*) Janos Levente/Shutterstock, (*center*) Sofi photo/Shutterstock; **49** ©Masterfile Royalty Free; **50** (*clockwise from top left*) Suprijono Suharjoto/Thinkstock, Blend Images/SuperStock, Jack Hollingsworth/Thinkstock, Jupiterimages/Thinkstock; **53** ©Mitchell Funk/Photographer's Choice/Getty Images; **56** ©Stockbyte/Thinkstock; **59** (*left to right*) ©Enrique Algarra/age fotostock, ©Dan Brownsword/Cultura/Getty Images, ©Masterfile Royalty Free; **63** ©Vicki Reid/E+/Getty Images; **68** ©Iakov Kalinin/Shutterstock; **70** Arvind Balaraman/Thinkstock; **71** (*left to right*) ©Greg Epperson/Shutterstock, ©Image Source/age fotostock; **Back cover:** (*clockwise from top*) ©Leszek Bogdewicz/Shutterstock, ©Wavebreak Media/Thinkstock, ©Blend Images/Alamy, ©limpido/Shutterstock

Text credits

The authors and publishers acknowledge the following sources of copyright material and are grateful for the permissions granted. While every effort has been made, it has not always been possible to identify the sources of all the material used, or to trace all copyright holders. If any omissions are brought to our notice, we will be happy to include the appropriate acknowledgments on reprinting.

48 Adapted from "Everyday Creativity," by Carlin Flora, *Psychology Today,* November 1, 2009. Psychology Today © Copyright 2005, www.Psychologytoday.com; **54** Adapted from "Why We Dream: Real Reasons Revealed," by Rachael Rettner, *LiveScience,* June 27, 2010. Reproduced with permission of LiveScience; **60** Adapted from "The Survival Guide for Dealing with Chronic Complainers," by Guy Winch, PhD, *Psychology Today,* July 15, 2011. Reproduced with permission of Guy Winch, www.guywinch.com; **66** Adapted from "Internet On, Inhibitions Off: Why We Tell All," by Matt Ridley, *The Wall Street Journal,* February 18, 2012. Reproduced with permission of The Wall Street Journal. Copyright © 2012 Dow Jones & Company, Inc. All Rights Reserved Worldwide; **72** Adapted from "International Careers: A World of Opportunity: Battling Culture Shock Starts with Trip to Local Bookstores, Seminars: Advance preparation is critical in adjusting to the challenges of life in a foreign country," by Karen E. Klein, *Los Angeles Times,* September 11, 1995. Copyright © 1995. Los Angeles Times. Reprinted with permission.

LESSON **A** ▶ *A weird, wired world*

1 VOCABULARY

Use the words and phrases in the box to complete the sentences.

app	the cloud	podcasts	text
blog	download	spyware	virus

1. This _____ *app* _____ lets me find the lowest price for gasoline from my phone.

2. Do you have Wi-Fi here? I need to _____ some files for work.

3. Now that I store everything in _____, I can access my data from anywhere.

4. If your device is running really slowly, it probably has a _____.

5. Cal writes opinion pieces about music and posts them on his _____.

6. Even though I moved abroad, I still listen to _____ of shows from my favorite hometown radio station online.

7. Many people find it's more convenient to _____ than to talk to people on the phone.

8. Some programs use _____ to gather private information without your knowledge.

2 GRAMMAR

One of the underlined words in each sentence is a mistake. Circle it and write the correct word in the blank.

1. In the near future, more cars will (been) driven by computers than by people. _____ *be* _____

2. More tablets are being using in the classroom all the time. _____

3. Medical data has going to be accessed online by both doctors and patients. _____

4. More songs have be downloaded this year than ever before. _____

5. All laptops in the store have being priced to sell quickly. _____

6. More and more TV shows having been made available through apps. _____

7. Increasingly, shopping and banking will be do on portable devices. _____

8. Smartphones are going to been designed with even more features. _____

VOCABULARY

Choose the connector that best completes each sentence.

1. Nat dropped his phone on the sidewalk yesterday. *Nevertheless /* *As a result*, it doesn't work anymore.

2. Parents should monitor the websites their children visit. *Additionally / On the other hand*, they need to talk to their children about Internet safety.

3. Cell phones are becoming more advanced. Some, *for instance / likewise*, have many of the capabilities of a computer.

4. Penny switched Internet service providers to save money. *Furthermore / In fact*, she's now spending $15 less each month.

5. I really don't like having a TV in my apartment. *Similarly / On the other hand*, it's useful to have one when I have friends over.

6. Higher education has become much more common due to technology. *For example / Therefore*, my cousin completed her degree online while living in another country.

GRAMMAR

Use the passive of the present continuous and your own information to complete the sentences.

1. Blogs *are being written by just about everybody these days!* _____

2. An increasing number of devices _____

3. Many online classes _____

4. Some spyware _____

5. More and more apps _____

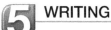

5 WRITING

A Read the review of an online course. Underline and number the passages where the author of the review does the following things.

1. names and explains the service
2. explains where the service is offered
3. mentions positive features
4. suggests how it could be improved
5. states who would find it useful and why

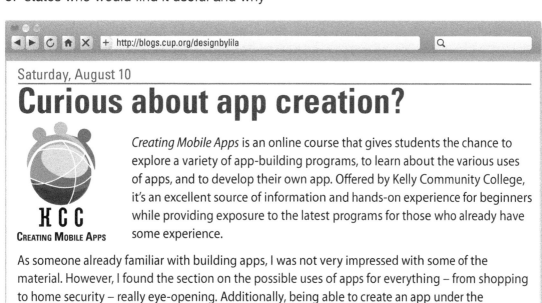

http://blogs.cup.org/designbylila

Saturday, August 10

Curious about app creation?

КСС
CREATING MOBILE APPS

Creating Mobile Apps is an online course that gives students the chance to explore a variety of app-building programs, to learn about the various uses of apps, and to develop their own app. Offered by Kelly Community College, it's an excellent source of information and hands-on experience for beginners while providing exposure to the latest programs for those who already have some experience.

As someone already familiar with building apps, I was not very impressed with some of the material. However, I found the section on the possible uses of apps for everything – from shopping to home security – really eye-opening. Additionally, being able to create an app under the guidance of an expert made the whole process seem much simpler than expected. Overall, it provided a flexible learning experience, and I found that the biggest advantage of an online class is that you can move at your own pace. On the other hand, there's the obvious lack of real time spent with the instructor and fellow students.

I would definitely recommend this course to anyone looking to build an app. My only suggestion is that the college should offer better networking tools so that the discussions and brainstorming sessions are more efficient.

B Use one of these topics or your own idea to write a product or service review.

- a course you took
- a social networking site
- software you tried

_____

_____

_____

_____

_____

_____

_____

_____

_____

_____

LESSON B ▶ *Information overload*

1 VOCABULARY

Use the words and phrases in the box to complete the sentences.

banner ads	bumper sticker	infomercial	spam	text messages
billboard	crawl	pop-up ads	telemarketing	voice mail

1. Have you seen that funny ad for a tablet on a huge _____*billboard*_____ on the highway?

2. A(n) _____ is a long commercial that looks like a TV show.

3. I'm not sure how effective _____ is. I never answer calls from numbers I don't recognize.

4. The _____ at the bottom of the TV screen said a storm was coming.

5. If I don't answer my phone, just leave me a _____.

6. I rarely see _____ on my computer because my browser blocks them really well.

7. I find _____ really annoying when they appear everywhere on a blog I'm reading.

8. All _____ email I receive is sent to a separate folder that gets automatically cleared once a week.

9. I'm uncomfortable talking on my phone in public, so I prefer to send _____.

10. The car in front of me had a _____ that said, "I'm not driving too fast – I sure hope you aren't!"

2 GRAMMAR

Complete these negative questions or tag questions with *doesn't, don't, isn't, shouldn't,* or *wouldn't.*

1. __*Don't*__ you think that there are lots of great cooking sites online?

2. _____ it be terrific if Wi-Fi were free for everyone?

3. Sam's probably in a meeting. It's better to leave him a voice mail, _____ it?

4. _____ Sheila register for classes online before they fill up?

5. _____ it seem like it's impossible to keep up with your social networking accounts at times?

6. Computer viruses are getting more sophisticated, _____ you think?

7. _____ it strange that no one has sent me any email today?

8. Banner ads get really annoying when they take up too much of the screen, _____ they?

GRAMMAR

Rewrite the sentences in two ways using negative questions and tag questions and the words in parentheses.

1. It's amazing how much time someone can waste online. (isn't)
   Isn't it amazing how much time someone can waste online?
   It's amazing how much time someone can waste online, isn't it?

2. It would be great to get a bus wrap to advertise our business. (wouldn't)
   _____
   _____

3. Students should try to avoid sending text messages during class. (shouldn't)
   _____
   _____

4. It seems like new technologies are being invented every day. (doesn't)
   _____
   _____

5. It's annoying that some ads move all over the computer screen. (isn't)
   _____
   _____

6. It's amazing how some people can watch infomercials for hours. (don't you think)
   _____
   _____

GRAMMAR

Write negative questions or tag questions about things you can do online.
Choose from the items in the box or use your own ideas.

shopping
reading the news
watching videos
planning a vacation
making new friends
looking for a job

1. *It's so convenient to shop online nowadays, isn't it?* _____
2. _____
3. _____
4. _____
5. _____
6. _____

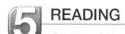

READING

A Read the blog post. Find the boldfaced words that match these definitions.

1. prepared; having no objection ___*willing*___
2. someone you know, but not well _____
3. invited to connect on a social network _____
4. accidents _____
5. are grateful for _____
6. at the same time _____

Are You **Tech** Obsessed?

Tuesday, February 2

Most of us **appreciate** the convenience of our tech devices, but for some people, it goes beyond a healthy appreciation. Take this quiz about tech obsession. How many of these are true for you?

1. Do you ever have **mishaps** because you are using your device while walking?

2. Are you **willing** to wait in line for more than 12 hours to get the latest version of a device?

3. Do you wake up in the middle of the night to check all your social networking accounts?

4. Do you text your friends even when they are in the same room?

5. Do you ever watch different shows on your phone, tablet, and TV **simultaneously**?

6. Do you check your phone continuously when you're out with friends or family at a movie, a sporting event, or a restaurant?

7. Do you change your device covers all the time? Are you one of the millions who love choosing new "fashions" for their devices?

8. Do you use online slang when you're offline? For example, you might say about a new **acquaintance**, "I **friended** him in English class last week."

This quiz was pretty funny, don't you think? Unfortunately, I answered "yes" to seven of the questions! How about you? Are you tech obsessed like me?

Posted by Walker White at 5:36 p.m.

B Read the statements. Do you think the author of the blog post would say these behaviors are obsessive or not obsessive? Choose the correct answer.

	Obsessive	Not obsessive
1. You have to be reminded to check your device for calls and messages.	☐	☑
2. People don't always understand you because you use a lot of online slang.	☐	☐
3. You often trip and fall in the street because you're checking email on your phone.	☐	☐
4. You have been using the same version of your device for several years.	☐	☐
5. You have a huge collection of colorful covers for your devices.	☐	☐
6. You turn off your device when you're with friends.	☐	☐

LESSON A ▶ *Exploring creativity*

1 GRAMMAR

Rewrite the sentences by making the reduced clauses into full clauses.

1. A person with great cooking and business skills would make a good restaurant owner.
   A person who has great cooking and business skills would make a
   good restaurant owner.

2. Those able to think creatively are the best team leaders.
   _____

3. A person opening a new business should try unusual marketing methods.
   _____

4. People with musical skills should share their talent with others.
   _____

5. People hoping to succeed in the arts should be prepared for financial challenges.
   _____

2 GRAMMAR

Reduce each relative clause. Then complete the sentences with your own ideas.

1. A person who is living on a tight budget . . .
   A person living on a tight budget shouldn't eat out too often.

2. Anyone who is interested in becoming a doctor . . .
   _____

3. Someone who is considering an artistic career . . .
   _____

4. People who are able to work at home . . .
   _____

5. A supervisor who has too much work to do . . .
   _____

6. A person who is required to take a foreign language in school . . .
   _____

7. People who are becoming bored with their jobs . . .
   _____

VOCABULARY

A Write the nouns that relate to the adjectives.

1. curious _____curiosity_____
2. decisive _____
3. determined _____
4. disciplined _____
5. innovative _____
6. knowledgeable _____

7. motivated _____
8. original _____
9. passionate _____
10. patient _____
11. perceptive _____
12. resourceful _____

B Now write sentences about these people using adjectives and nouns from above.

1. business executive _A knowledgeable person who has innovative ideas_
   might make a good business executive.

2. web designer _____
   _____

3. journalist _____
   _____

4. lawyer _____
   _____

GRAMMAR

What qualities are needed to do these jobs? Use reduced relative clauses in your answers.

singer   **landscaper**   **architect**

1. _A person considering_   2. _____   3. _____

   becoming a singer needs   _____   _____

   _to be_ _____   _____   _____

   _____   _____   _____

   _____   _____   _____

   _____   _____   _____

WRITING

A Read Erica's story. Choose the word or words you would use to describe her.

☐ curious ☐ determined ☐ original ☐ resourceful

If you've ever planned a big event, something like this may have happened to you, but I certainly never thought it would happen to me! My fiancé and I were planning to get married in six months when his company decided to transfer him overseas – in two weeks! He wouldn't be able to return to the U.S. for some time, which meant we couldn't get married as planned. I told a friend about this, and she said, "So get married now!" I reminded her that there was no time to plan anything. She responded, "Then get creative." So I did. First, I designed and sent out email invitations. Then, as there was no time to book a venue, we decided to have both the ceremony and reception in my parents' backyard. My mother put together the decorations, which were flowering plants in pots. A friend of mine who's a chef prepared the food, and we had lots of cupcakes instead of a big cake. The clothes were the biggest challenge; there wasn't any time to make a new dress as I had planned. Luckily, I remembered the dress I'd made for a project in college. With a few alterations, it was perfect. I asked my three bridesmaids to wear dresses they already had – in any color. In the end, the wedding was fantastic thanks to everyone putting their creativity to work.

B Read the story again. Write a *P* where you think each new paragraph should begin.

C Write a three-paragraph composition about a problem you actually had or imagine you might have. How did you or would you solve the problem?

If you _____, something like this may have happened to you, but I certainly never thought it would happen to me. _____

_____

_____

_____

_____

_____

_____

_____

_____

1 VOCABULARY

Choose the word that best completes each sentence.

1. Seat belts alone did not protect car passengers enough, which is why researchers (found)/ *made* / *solved* a safer solution: air bags for cars.

2. You need to *explore* / *organize* / *solve* your information before you present it to other people. Otherwise, they won't understand it.

3. Our report *explored* / *made* / *solved* several possibilities for increasing the car's efficiency.

4. The board of directors *analyzed* / *found* / *organized* the alternatives carefully when they chose a new location for the research facility.

5. It's important to consider many solutions when you are *making* / *organizing* / *solving* a problem.

6. Our science experiment didn't work. We *explored* / *made* / *solved* a mistake in the calculations.

43050Z02

2 GRAMMAR

Read the conversation. Find the mistakes in the underlined sentences, and rewrite them so that they are correct. The mistake might be use of commas.

A: Why are we leaving so early? The meeting doesn't start for another 30 minutes!

B: At this time of day, the traffic is terrible! (1) It moves at only about 20 miles an hour, that means we need to leave now.

A: Why don't we take public transportation?

B: (2) The buses are even slower which is why people avoid using them.

A: Then how about walking? (3) The office is a short distance from here, which it means that it shouldn't take long.

B: True. (4) And we can get some exercise, too, it is great!

1. *It moves at only about 20 miles an hour, which means (that) we need to leave now.*

2. _____

_____

3. _____

_____

4. _____

_____

3 GRAMMAR

Write sentences about these topics. Use non-defining relative clauses beginning with *which is why* or *which means (that).*

the common cold   *ATM*   *video chatting*   *pollution*

1. There is no cure for the common cold, *which is why researchers are working to find one.*

2. ATMs are available everywhere, _____

   _____

3. Video chatting is easy for almost everyone, _____

   _____

4. Pollution has become less of a problem in many cities, _____

   _____

4 GRAMMAR

Combine the sentences with non-defining relative clauses beginning with *which is why,* *which means (that),* or *which is* + adjective.

1. People feel the need to keep in touch. Social networking sites are popular.

   People feel the need to keep in touch, which is why social networking sites are popular.

2. New diseases are being discovered all the time. Researchers have to work even harder.

   _____

3. Some people like listening to music on vinyl records. It's strange to me.

   _____

4. Traffic congestion is becoming a major problem in cities. New types of public transportation will have to be developed.

   _____

5. Reality TV shows are cheap and easy to produce. There are so many of them now.

   _____

A Read the article quickly. Choose the best title for the article.

☐ Some People Will Never Be Creative ☐ How to Become an Artist

☐ What Everyday Creativity Means

When we think of creativity, we think of Mozart, Picasso, Einstein – people with a combination of talent and opportunity. But the truth is that all sorts of people are capable of engaging in creative processes. Just because you don't plan to be a famous actor or choreographer doesn't mean that you can't use your natural creativity and make your life your own masterpiece.

Zorana Ivcevic, a psychologist who studies creativity, has found that while some people fit into more traditional creative roles, as dancers or scientists, many others express their creativity through more routine acts. She also found that certain personality traits are shared by the "officially" creative and those who practice everyday creativity. Both groups tend to be open-minded and curious, and they are persistent, positive, energetic, and motivated by their chosen activities. And while 30 percent of the people studied showed no signs of creativity, they shouldn't lose hope. Other studies show that taking up creative pursuits actually makes people more flexible and less judgmental.

Experts at the Harvard Medical School define everyday creativity as expressions of originality and meaningfulness. Rebecca Whitlinger provided an example of this when she decided to make use of her seemingly useless collection of bridesmaid dresses. She resolved to wear them everywhere and asked friends to take snapshots of her wearing them in many unlikely situations, even while parasailing. Then it occurred to her to turn this idea into a fundraising event for a charity she worked for. Guests were asked to wear outfits they would be unable to wear again (such as a bridesmaid dress). Creative? Yes. Meaningful? Well, the fundraiser made $90,000 in its first few years.

"It's too bad that, when considering what endeavors may be creative, people immediately think of the arts," says Michele Root-Bernstein, co-author of *Sparks of Genius*. "It's the problem-solving processes they exhibit rather than the content or craft that make them so. Just about anything we do can be addressed in a creative manner, from housecleaning to personal hobbies to work."

B Read the article again. Choose the answers that best reflect the ideas in the article.

1. According to Zorana Ivcevic, how many people naturally show signs of creativity?

☐ a. everyone ☐ b. more people than most of us think ☐ c. very few people

2. According to the article, which of these personality traits is not as commonly linked to creativity?

☐ a. impatience ☐ b. optimism ☐ c. curiosity

3. Rebecca Whitlinger had the idea for a fundraising event when she . . .

☐ a. joined a charity. ☐ b. took up photography. ☐ c. creatively reused some clothes.

4. Michele Root-Bernstein believes that creativity can be . . .

☐ a. found in everything we do. ☐ b. found only in the arts. ☐ c. hard to define.

GENERALLY SPEAKING

LESSON A ► *How typical are you?*

GRAMMAR

Choose the expression that best completes each sentence.

1. (*Unlike*)/ *While* many Americans, people in my country do not watch a lot of TV.
2. *In contrast to* / *While* many of my friends eat meat, I'm a vegetarian.
3. Monica is a typical teenager, *unlike* / *except for the fact that* she likes to get up early in the morning.
4. *Unlike* / *While* lots of my friends, I spend very little time on my phone.
5. I'm similar to people my age, *while* / *except that* I don't live at home.
6. *Unlike* / *While* most of my classmates, I prefer walking home to taking the bus.
7. Students in my country are just like other teens, *unlike* / *except that* we sometimes have to go to school on Saturdays.
8. I like all kinds of music, *except that* / *except for* jazz.

VOCABULARY

Use the words and phrases in the box to complete the sentences.

| amenable |
| conform to |
| conservative |
| fits in |
| follows the crowd |
| make waves |
| rebellious |
| unconventional |

1. Emma _____*fits in*_____ easily with the other girls in her college.
2. I don't mind working overtime. I'm actually quite _____ to it.
3. Neil likes to do his own thing. He doesn't _____ other people's ideas.
4. Sam does the opposite of what people tell him to do. He's very _____.
5. My town is very resistant to change. It's quite _____.
6. Sadie always goes along with her friends' plans. She doesn't like to _____.
7. Jake has _____ ideas about his work. He tries to be original.
8. My cousin usually _____ when it comes to fashion. She likes to dress exactly like her friends.

3 GRAMMAR

Read these descriptions of people. Who are you similar to or different from?
Write sentences using *unlike, while, in contrast to, except that, except for,*
and *except for the fact that.*

What are you like ?

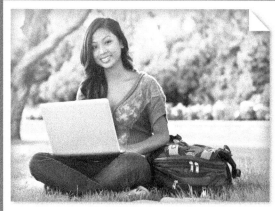

I am a college sophomore, and my major is
English literature. My interests include tennis,
reading, and travel. I enjoy exploring new
places – especially places few people visit.
— KIM

Hi! I love music of all kinds, and I play guitar
in a band. I love loud music – the louder the
better. I'm interested in musical instruments,
and I enjoy collecting them.
— MARIA

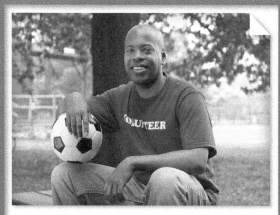

I am a 25-year-old computer science
student. I am very interested in technology
and soccer. I love building computers in my
spare time.
— DONALD

Do you like visiting historical sites? Do you
enjoy reading books about history? I do. I am
23 and an accountant, but my real passion is
history. I also enjoy collecting rare coins.
— LUIS

1. *I have a lot in common with Kim, except that I don't like sports.*

2. _____

3. _____

4. _____

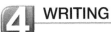

WRITING

A Read these paragraphs and answer the questions.

More and more Americans are living alone nowadays. While an increasing number of people end up living alone because of varying life circumstances, such as a change in marital status, more people are choosing to live alone today than in the past. According to a recent U.S. census, 28 percent of all households in the United States are made up of just one person. This is a dramatic change from the extended families of just a couple of generations ago.

1. What is the topic sentence?

   _____

2. What reasons are given to support the topic sentence?

   _____

   _____

3. What fact is given to support the topic sentence?

   _____

The typical American living alone is neither old nor lonely. In fact, about 5 million people between the ages of 18 and 34 live alone, and the majority of them have chosen to do so. They are acting on a desire to be more independent, and they often have a more varied social life.

4. What is the topic sentence?

   _____

5. What fact is given to support the topic sentence?

   _____

6. What reasons are given to support the topic sentence?

   _____

   _____

B Choose the topic sentence below that you like best. Then add at least four supporting statements to make a complete paragraph.

- It is *unusual / typical* for young people in my country to live alone.
- It is *easy / difficult* to get into college in my country.

_____

_____

_____

_____

_____

GRAMMAR

Complete the blog post with *used to* or *would* and the words in the box. Sometimes more than one answer is possible.

like	listen	not be	not turn on	play	save	watch

http://blogs.cup.org/ryansreflections

Sunday, March 14

I had a funny conversation with my grandfather the other day. He was telling me what things were like when he was a kid. First of all, there (1) _____ ***didn't use to be*** _____ any technology like tablets, smartphones, or handheld game consoles to entertain him. When he wanted to hear music, he (2) _____ to the radio, or he (3) _____ a record on a record player. He did have a TV, but he (4) _____ it only at night. He (5) _____ the TV during the day because there were only four channels, and the programs were boring in the daytime. He also said he (6) _____ reading mystery and suspense novels. He (7) _____ his allowance to buy his favorite books. I feel kind of bad for my granddad – it doesn't sound like the most exciting childhood.

 VOCABULARY

Complete the conversation with *keep* or *stay*. Sometimes more than one answer is possible.

Lola: Mrs. Wu's class is so difficult! I'm always up late studying for her class, so I can barely (1) _____ ***stay*** _____ awake the next morning. I don't know how I'll survive the semester!

Max: Yeah, I remember how demanding Mrs. Wu can be. My best advice is to (2) _____ up with the work you need to do each day. And don't procrastinate!

Lola: That's good advice. Her assignments are long and complicated. I always worry I won't be able to (3) _____ my grades up in her class!

Max: Even though you're stressed out, try to (4) _____ things in perspective. Also, if you let her know that you'll do what it takes to get good grades, maybe she'll help you (5) _____ out of trouble.

Lola: That's a good idea. I'll talk to Mrs. Wu tomorrow. And I'll (6) _____ in touch with you to let you know how things go.

3 GRAMMAR

Rewrite each sentence using the past habitual with *used to* or *would*. If there are two possibilities, write them both.

1. James was a very good chess player when he was younger.
   James used to be a very good chess player when he was younger.

2. In college, my friends and I studied for our tests together at the library.
   _____

3. I always asked my older sister for help with my science homework.
   _____

4. My English teacher didn't assign work over holidays or long weekends.
   _____

5. Rowan lived in an apartment near the university.
   _____

6. Carrie emailed her mom every day when she went away to school.
   _____

4 GRAMMAR

Complete the sentences with *used to* or *would* and information that is true for you.

1. Three years ago, I _____ *used to* _____ live
   in a very noisy apartment on a noisy
   city street.

2. Last summer, my friends and I _____
   _____
   _____
   _____

3. When I was younger, I _____ go to
   _____
   _____
   _____

4. A friend of mine _____ have trouble in _____
   class because _____

5. My favorite teacher was _____. He/She _____
   _____

6. When I was first learning English, I _____
   _____

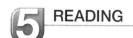

5 READING

A Read the article quickly. What is Deirdre Barrett's main theory on dreaming?

YOUR **DREAMS** CAN HELP SOLVE YOUR DAY'S **PROBLEMS**

The slumbering mind might not seem like the best tool for critical thinking, but according to recent research, humans can actually solve problems while asleep. In fact, one purpose for dreaming may be to help us find solutions to puzzles that bother us while we're awake. Dreams are highly visual and often illogical, which makes them useful for the type of "out-of-the-box" thinking that some problem solving requires, explained Deirdre Barrett, a psychologist at Harvard University. Barrett's theory on dreaming boils down to this: Dreaming is really just thinking, but in a slightly different state from when our eyes are open.

Barrett has studied problem solving in dreams for more than 10 years and has documented many examples of the phenomenon in this time. In one experiment, Barrett asked college students to pick a homework problem to try to solve while sleeping. Students focused on the problem each night before they went to bed. At the end of a week, about half of the students had dreamed about the problem, and about a quarter had had a dream that contained the answer.

Having extensively reviewed scientific and historical literature for examples of problems solved in dreams, Barrett also found almost every type of problem being solved, from the mathematical to the artistic. Many were problems that required the individual to visualize something in his or her mind, such as an inventor picturing a new device. The other major category of problems solved included "ones where the conventional wisdom is just wrong about how to approach the problem," Barrett said. She added that dreams might have developed to be particularly good at allowing us to work out puzzles that fall into these two categories. "It's just extra thinking time," she stressed – though it's time that allows us to think in more flexible and creative ways.

$$e = mc^2$$
$$dS \geq 0$$
$$a^2 + b^2 = c^2$$
$$\pi = c/d$$

B Read the article again. Are the statements true or false? Choose the correct answer. Then rewrite the false statements to make them true.

	True	False
1. The creative thinking associated with dreams makes them good for some types of problem solving.	☐	☐
2. Barrett has only recently begun studying dreams.	☐	☐
3. The students in Barrett's experiment all solved their problems while asleep.	☐	☐
4. According to Barrett, only certain kinds of problems can be solved while dreaming.	☐	☐
5. Inventors may find dreams particularly useful.	☐	☐

10 THE ART OF COMPLAINING

LESSON **A** ▶ *That really bugs me!*

1 GRAMMAR

Use the clauses in the box to complete the sentences.

how quickly the battery runs down · when my favorite show is interrupted by a news bulletin · people who make noise when they eat · who honk their horns all the time · waiting a long time to be seated · why people push in front of me in line · water dripping in the sink

1. The thing that really bothers me at the dinner table is . . .

   The thing that really bothers me at the dinner table is people who make noise when they eat.

2. When I'm trying to sleep at night, something that irks me is . . .

3. One thing I can't understand in the supermarket is . . .

4. The thing that really irritates me when I go to a restaurant is . . .

5. Something I can't stand is drivers . . .

6. Something that bothers me about my new cell phone is . . .

7. When I'm watching TV, one thing that bugs me is . . .

2 GRAMMAR

Write sentences about things that irritate you. Use relative clauses and noun clauses, and your own ideas.

1. *The thing that bothers me at the dinner table is when people talk with their mouths full.*

2.

3.

4.

3 GRAMMAR

Use relative clauses and noun clauses to write about everyday annoyances in these places.

on the road   **in the park**   **in the library**   **on the subway**

1. *The thing that annoys me on the road is when other drivers follow too closely.*

2. _____

3. _____

4. _____

4 VOCABULARY

Choose the word that best completes each sentence. Sometimes more than one answer is possible.

1. One thing that *drives* /(*gets*)/ *makes* me down is when it rains on the weekend.

2. Something that *drives* / *gets* / *makes* me up the wall is when I have to wait on a long line to buy one or two items.

3. The thing that *drives* / *gets* / *makes* my blood boil is when my sister borrows my clothes.

4. One thing that *drives* / *gets* / *makes* me upset is when people are rude to store clerks for no reason.

5. The one thing that *drives* / *gets* / *makes* under my skin is when someone's cell phone rings during a movie or play.

6. When I'm talking to someone, the thing that *drives* / *gets* / *makes* on my nerves is when he or she keeps interrupting me.

7. My sister sending text messages during dinner *drives* / *gets* / *makes* me crazy.

8. One thing my brother does that *drives* / *gets* / *makes* me sick is when he leaves piles of dirty dishes in the kitchen sink.

WRITING

A Read the email complaining about a service. Number the four paragraphs in a logical order.

To: customerservice@bestgym.cup.com

Subject: Complaint about personal training service

To whom it may concern:

My trainer, Dan, has not arrived on time for a single 6:00 a.m. session. The earliest he has arrived is 6:15, and several times he has come at 6:30. I am paying extra for his services, and I am certainly not getting my money's worth. Dan also tends to wander off while I am exercising, getting involved in conversations with other gym employees. My understanding was that he would carefully supervise my training, which he has not done.

When I signed up for the program, the head trainer and I sat down, discussed my problems and needs, and drew up a plan, which was signed by both of us. This will show clearly what my expectations were in case you need to see this in writing. However, I hope it's clear by now that my needs have not been met.

I would like you to assign me a new trainer or refund my fee for the personal training service. If you can't do this by next week, I will take my business to another gym.

I am writing to complain about the personal trainer who was recently assigned to me at your gym. I signed up for six weeks of the intensive training program, including an individual fitness evaluation, and I am extremely dissatisfied.

Sincerely,
Elizabeth Smith
212-555-0199

B Use the numbers you wrote for the paragraphs above to answer these questions. In which paragraph does the writer . . .

a. explain the problem in detail? _____

b. explain what she wants? _____

c. describe the type of service clearly? _____

d. mention evidence of a service contract? _____

C Write an email complaining about a problem regarding a service or product you are not satisfied with.

To whom it may concern:

_____

_____

_____

_____

_____

_____

_____

GRAMMAR

Write *S* for a simple indirect question and *C* for a complex indirect question.

_S_ 1. I want to find out how to use less fat in my cooking.

___ 2. Why people aren't concerned about the crime rate is a mystery to me.

___ 3. I wonder if other people are concerned about the pollution problems in our city.

___ 4. The thing I don't get is why food prices are so high.

___ 5. One of my concerns is whether I will be able to afford a new car.

___ 6. I'd like to know if the weather will be nice this weekend.

___ 7. How some people can listen to such loud music is something I can't understand.

___ 8. I want to know when a cure for the common cold will be discovered.

GRAMMAR

Use the phrases in parentheses to rewrite the questions.

1. Why are the trains running so slowly? (. . . is a mystery to me.)
   Why the trains are running so slowly is a mystery to me.

2. Will there be cheaper health care for employees? (One of my concerns . . .)
   _____

3. Why do I get so much junk mail? (. . . is something I can't understand.)
   _____

4. How can you eat so much and not feel sick? (What I don't get . . .)
   _____

5. Who should I call if I don't get my passport on time? (I wonder . . .)
   _____

6. Will politicians do more to help the environment? (I'd like to know . . .)
   _____

7. Why don't people turn off their cell phones when they're at the movies?
   (. . . is beyond me.)
   _____

8. Why can't James get to work on time? (. . . is the thing that concerns me.)
   _____

9. Why do I get a cold every summer? (. . . is a mystery to me.)
   _____

10. Did someone use my tablet while I was out of the room? (I want to find out . . .)
    _____

VOCABULARY

Choose the word that best completes each sentence.

1. Lena was *infuriated* / *insulted* when she missed her flight due to the traffic jam.
2. John was very *irritated* / *saddened* to hear about the house that had been damaged by the storm.
3. Vicky was *depressed* / *mystified* when the forecast called for rain on her wedding day.
4. The players on the football team were *humiliated* / *insulted* when they lost the championship game by 22 points.
5. We were absolutely *demoralized* / *stunned* when we found out we had won the prize.
6. Chiang was totally *baffled* / *discouraged* when a complete stranger started talking to him as if they were old friends.
7. Joan was *enraged* / *discouraged* when she saw that someone had damaged her car and not even left a note for her.
8. June became pretty *insulted* / *annoyed* when her Wi-Fi kept disconnecting.

GRAMMAR

Write sentences about each urban problem below or about ideas of your own.

| transportation | sanitation | parking |

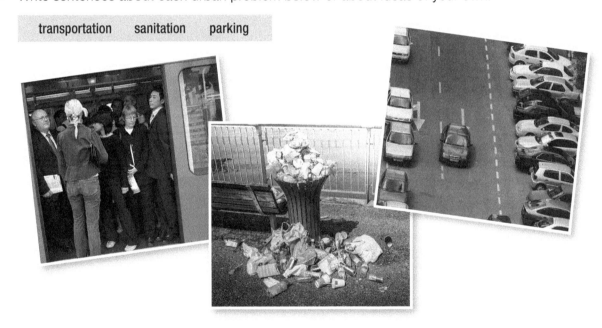

1. I don't know *why bus service is so infrequent. It's almost impossible to get to work on time.*

2. It's beyond me _____

3. I wonder _____

4. My big concern _____

A Read the article quickly. Write the number of each section next to its title.

_____ a. Understanding What Chronic Complainers Want

_____ b. Understanding What Chronic Complainers Don't Want

_____ c. Understanding How Chronic Complainers Think

The Survival Guide For Dealing With Chronic Complainers

*Optimists see a glass half full. Pessimists see a glass half empty. Chronic complainers see a glass that is slightly **chipped**, holding water that isn't cold enough, probably because it's tap water when they asked for bottled.*

The constant negativity of chronic complainers presents a challenge for those around them. Trying to remain positive and productive when there's a constant stream of complaints can try anyone's patience. And trying to be helpful will only **backfire**. So here are some essential tips to help those who deal with chronic complainers on a daily basis.

1 Despite the **gloom**, complainers don't see themselves as negative people. They see *the world* as negative and themselves as responding to the unfortunate circumstances of their lives.

Survival Tip #1 Never try to convince complainers that things are "not as bad" as they seem. This will only encourage them to come up with 10 additional **misfortunes** that might help you understand how terrible their lives actually are.

2 Chronic complainers are looking for sympathy and emotional **validation**. All they really want is for you to tell them that, yes, they've gotten a bad deal, and you feel their pain – just not as much as they do.

Survival Tip #2 The quickest way to get away from a complainer is to express sympathy and then change the subject. For example, "The printer jammed on you again? Sorry! I know it's hard, but I hope you can be a trooper because we really have to get back to work."

3 The idea that chronic complainers' lives are filled with tragedy is a big part of their **sense of identity**. Therefore, even good advice is a threat, because what complainers really want is for you to know they are suffering. They will often tell you why your solution won't work or might even become upset because you don't understand how unsolvable their problems are.

Survival Tip #3 You should avoid offering advice or solutions and stick to sympathy. However, there are situations where a problem is obviously very real. In this case, offer sympathy followed by brief but clear advice, and it will probably be accepted and appreciated.

B Read the article. Find the boldfaced word that matches each definition.

1. lack of hope ___*gloom*___

2. bad things that happen _____

3. your idea of who you are _____

4. have the opposite effect to what was intended _____

5. damaged because a small piece has broken off _____

6. proof that something is true or real _____

VALUES

LESSON A ▶ *How honest are you?*

GRAMMAR

1 Complete the sentences with *even if, only if,* or *unless.*

1. I wouldn't interrupt a lesson _____*unless*_____ I had an important question.

2. I would leave the scene of a car accident _____ I knew for sure that no one was injured.

3. _____ I were really hungry, I still wouldn't take food that wasn't mine.

4. I would ask my neighbors to be more quiet in the morning _____ we had a good relationship.

5. I wouldn't ask to borrow a friend's phone _____ I knew he or she wouldn't mind.

6. _____ I didn't like my brother's new wife, I'd still be nice to her.

VOCABULARY

2 Choose the correct words to complete the sentences.

1. Steph won't mind if we rewrite parts of her article. She's very (agreeable) / *rational* to change.

2. It's *disapproving / unfair* that Mrs. Moore only blamed Lydia for the accident. Terry was responsible for the accident, too.

3. I'm sure Mark wasn't being *honest / irresponsible* when he said he liked my new shoes.

4. I can't believe Brianna wasn't fired from her job. Her *trustworthy / unscrupulous* business practices have cost this company thousands of dollars.

5. Min-hee is a good choice for club treasurer. She's good with money, and she's quite *unethical / responsible*.

6. In many places, it's *illegal / logical* to use a cell phone and drive at the same time.

3 GRAMMAR

Respond to what the first speaker says in each of these conversations.

1. A: If I found a friend's diary, I'd read it.

    B: Really? I wouldn't read it, even if _I were_
    really curious, because diaries are
    supposed to be private.

2. A: You should never give a friend your email password.

    B: I would give a friend my email password only if _____
    _____

3. A: If I heard someone spreading false information about a good friend, I wouldn't tell that friend about it.

    B: I wouldn't tell my friend about the false information unless _____
    _____

4. A: I would lend my best friend money if she needed it.

    B: I wouldn't lend my best friend a lot of money unless _____
    _____

4 GRAMMAR

How do you feel about these situations? Write sentences about them using *unless*, *only if*, or *even if*.

- recommending a friend's restaurant you don't consider very good
- lending money to someone you barely know
- giving fashion advice to a friend whose clothes you consider inappropriate
- saying you like a gift that you really don't like just to be nice

1. _I would never recommend a friend's restaurant that I don't consider very good_
   unless I knew he/she was trying to improve it.

2. _____
   _____

3. _____
   _____

4. _____
   _____

WRITING

A Read this composition and choose the best thesis statement.

☐ I am glad that I learned the importance of being responsible when I was young.

☐ I am thankful that I learned the importance of saving money when I was a child.

☐ I feel fortunate to have learned as a child how important family is.

_____ I grew up on a farm. My family had to care for the animals morning and evening, seven days a week. Even during school vacations and on weekends, there was work to be done, and each of my brothers and sisters had jobs that our parents depended on us to do.

For example, when I was 12, my parents entrusted me with the care of the young animals. That meant that if an animal was sick or injured, I had to take charge, giving the animal its medication and generally making sure it had a chance to get well. Most farmers had problems with their calves frequently getting sick. I was proud that my calves were usually healthy. That fact alone proved to me that I was doing a good job and making the right decisions.

Another way I learned responsibility is that, from the age of 12, I was paid for my work. Because I was working hard for my own money, I learned how to budget and save. When I was 14, I was able to buy a 10-speed bicycle with my savings. And because I demonstrated how responsible I was, by the time I was 16, my parents trusted me enough to help with the farm accounts.

In conclusion, being allowed to make important decisions and take charge of my own finances at an early age taught me what being responsible really means. Now, in my working life, I know that if I take care of the jobs that are given to me, my colleagues will see they can trust me with even more challenging tasks in the future.

B Now write a composition about something you learned as a child that is useful to you now. Begin the paragraphs as indicated below.

I'm glad that I learned _____

_____

_____

For example, _____

_____

_____

Another way I learned _____

_____

_____

In conclusion, _____

_____

_____

GRAMMAR

Complete the sentences with the correct form of the verbs in parentheses.

1.   Jay: I'm taking a French class at the community college.

     Meryl: I wish I _____*had*_____ (have) more time to learn a second language.

2.   Diego: I have to study tonight.

     Jim: If you _____ (study) yesterday, you would have been able to go to the concert with me tonight!

3. Camila: If only our neighbor _____ (play) his music more softly at night!

     Derek: I know. I haven't had a good night's sleep since he moved in!

4.   Rohan: Our boss is going to be upset when he sees what you've done.

     Julie: It's true. If I had been careful, I _____ (not spill) my drink on my computer.

5.   Albin: You look exhausted. Why don't you stop working for a few minutes?

     Lily: I wish I _____ (take) a break, but I have too much to do!

6.   Hiroto: I'm so glad you didn't get caught in that snowstorm!

     Kay: If you _____ (not warn) me, I probably would have gotten stuck on the road.

GRAMMAR

Complete the sentences with wishes and regrets about the illustration.
Use the phrases from the box.

forget my umbrella	check the weather forecast
wear my raincoat	find a taxi

1. I wish _*I hadn't forgotten my umbrella.*_

   _____

2. If only _____

   _____

3. I wish _____

   _____

4. If only _____

   _____

3 VOCABULARY

Use the words in the box to complete the sentences.

| compassionate | generous | resilient | selfish |
| discreet | indifference | respect | tolerance |

1. Even though Mr. Soto gave a _____*generous*_____ donation to the library fund, he wishes he could have given more.

2. If I had been more _____, Jenny wouldn't have found out about her surprise birthday party.

3. Make sure to be on time for your appointment with Ms. Benson. She doesn't have much _____ for lateness.

4. We lost all _____ for Ben when he lied about what happened to the computer.

5. I think it's important to teach children to be _____ toward others.

6. Gina is pretty _____. Even though she lost the singing competition, she'll be ready to sing again tomorrow.

7. _____ to global warming really bothers me.

8. Brad is so _____. He only thinks about how things affect him.

4 GRAMMAR

Read each situation. Then write one sentence with a wish about the present or future and one sentence with a regret about the past.

1. Tim stopped at a store to get a soda. He put his wallet down on the counter. When he went to pick it up, the wallet was gone! His ID and credit cards were in the wallet.

   Tim wishes he could find his wallet.

   If Tim hadn't set his wallet down, he wouldn't have lost his credit cards.

2. Laura had a 5:00 flight. She planned to take the 3:45 bus to the airport. Unfortunately, the bus was late. She missed her flight.

   _____

   _____

3. Charles was planning to study for four hours for his driver's test the next day. He went to the movies with his friend instead and studied for only 20 minutes. He failed the test.

   _____

   _____

4. Maxine quit going to college in her junior year. She planned to take one year off to travel and then go back to school. That was five years ago.

   _____

   _____

A Read the article quickly. Decades ago, what was the assumption about how the Internet would affect people's honesty?

Internet On, Inhibitions Off:
Why We Tell All On The Net

It is now well known that people are generally accurate and (sometimes embarrassingly) honest about their personalities when profiling themselves on social networking sites. Patients are willing to be more open about psychiatric symptoms to an automated online doctor than a real one. Pollsters find that people give more honest answers to an online survey than to one conducted by phone.

But online honesty cuts both ways. Bloggers find that readers who comment on their posts are often harshly frank, but that these same rude critics become polite if contacted directly. . . .

Why is this? Why do we become more honest the less we have to face each other? Posing the question may make the answer seem obvious – that we feel uncomfortable about confessing to or challenging others when face to face with them – but that begs the question: Why? This is one of those cases where it is helpful to compare human beings with other species, to set our behavior in context.

In many monkeys and apes, face-to-face contact is essentially antagonistic. Staring is a threat. . . . Put two monkey strangers in a cage and they keep well apart, avoid eye contact, and generally do their utmost to avoid triggering a fight. Put two people in an elevator and the same thing happens. . . .

For many primates, face-to-face contact carries a threat. When we're online, we're essentially faceless. Deep in our psyches, the act of writing a furious online critique of someone's views does not feel like a confrontation, whereas telling them the same thing over the phone or face to face does. All the cues are missing that would warn us not to risk a revenge attack by being too frank. . . .

Internet flaming and its benign equivalent, online honesty, are a surprise. Two decades ago, most people thought the anonymity of the online world would cause an epidemic of dishonesty, just as they thought it would lead to geeky social isolation. Then along came social networking, and the Internet not only turned social but became embarrassingly honest. . . .

B Read the article again. Choose the correct answers.

1. What do social networking sites and automated online doctors have in common?
   - ☐ a. They make people more honest.
   - ☐ b. They make people less trustworthy.
   - ☐ c. They make people more ethical.

2. A monkey that stands face-to-face with another monkey probably . . .
   - ☐ a. wants to be agreeable.
   - ☐ b. is showing respect.
   - ☐ c. is looking for a fight.

3. Why does the writer talk about monkeys and apes in the article?
   - ☐ a. To make a contrast with human behavior.
   - ☐ b. To help explain human behavior.
   - ☐ c. To point out animals are capable of dishonesty.

4. What does the author suggest is the cause of online frankness?
   - ☐ a. People have become less sociable.
   - ☐ b. It's human nature to confront others.
   - ☐ c. We don't feel threatened for saying what we think.

1 GRAMMAR

Look at the timeline that a mother has envisioned for her twins' lives. Are the sentences true or false? Choose the correct answer. Then rewrite the false sentences to make them true.

Max and Ava's Timeline

January 2010
born

September 2015
go to school for the first time

June 2032
graduate from college

August 2032
leave on a trip around the world

July 2035
return home from trip

October 2035
start their careers

	True	False
1. By September 2026, Max and Ava will have been going to school for 10 years.	☐	☑

By September 2026, Max and Ava will have been going to school for 11 years.

	True	False
2. By July 2032, they will already have graduated from college.	☐	☐
3. By September 2033, they will be leaving on a trip around the world.	☐	☐
4. By August 2035, they will have been traveling for three years.	☐	☐
5. It's now October 2034. By this time next year, they will have started their careers.	☐	☐
6. By October 2037, they will have been working for one year.	☐	☐

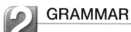

2 GRAMMAR

Complete the email. Use the future perfect or future perfect continuous of the verbs in parentheses.

To: Julie
Cc:
Subject: Paris!

Hi Julie,

By this time tomorrow, I (1) _____ **will have arrived** _____ (arrive) in France! I can't believe I get to study there! I'm nervous, but I hope by next week I (2) _____ (learn) my way around. I'm sure I (3) _____ (get) lost several times by then, too.

I (4) _____ (meet) my roommate by this time next week, too. I hope she's nice. I'm nervous about meeting my new classmates. They're all from different parts of the world. I hope in six month's time I (5) _____ (have) the opportunity to get to know each of them.

I can't wait for you to visit. Maybe you can come in December. That should give you some time to save money since you (6) _____ (work) for a few months by then. And also by then, I'm sure I (7) _____ (find) some great restaurants to eat at. I know how much you love French food!

I already miss you, so write to me as soon as you can!

Isabella

3 VOCABULARY

Complete the sentences with *about*, *in*, *of*, *to*, or *with*. Sometimes more than one answer is possible.

1. Kenji can't wait for his trip to the United States. He's looking forward _____ **to** _____ visiting California and New York.

2. Before Nicole left to work in her company's branch in Spain, she participated _____ a special training program.

3. If you have the opportunity to work in another country, don't be scared _____ taking it.

4. Michelle made friends easily after she adjusted _____ the new culture.

5. Jack was very excited _____ meeting his colleagues from China.

6. If you want to take advantage _____ your school's study abroad programs, you should talk to your adviser.

7. She wasn't familiar _____ the customs in her host country, but she soon adapted to life there.

8. As soon as he became aware _____ his company's policy allowing employees to work in another country for a year, he decided to apply.

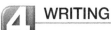

WRITING

A Read the three conclusions about the experience of working abroad. Write the letters of all the methods used in each conclusion.

a. looks to the future   c. summarizes the main points
b. concludes with the main idea   d. makes recommendations

b, c, d **1.** In conclusion, those who decide to live abroad gain experience of other cultures, understanding of others' work practices, and a deeper empathy for people of other countries. Working abroad widens your view of the world, and that will be of lasting benefit in both your work and personal life. Definitely do it if you can.

_____ **2.** To sum up, people who decide to work abroad will have the opportunity to change their lives in several ways. First, they will develop a deep understanding of another culture. Second, they will gain first-hand experience of work practices that can give them a new perspective on their own work. Last, they will broaden their knowledge of the world in ways that will stay with them for the rest of their lives.

_____ **3.** In brief, whether you decide to work abroad on a short-term basis or for an extended period, it is an experience that is educational, pleasurable, and practical. The experience allows you to flourish in all aspects of your life long after the experience is over and is highly recommended for anyone who has the chance to do it.

B Underline the words or phrases in each conclusion above that helped you decide which methods were used.

C Write a short essay about what people should expect to experience if they come to work or study in your country. Your conclusion should contain at least one of the methods listed above.

_____
_____
_____
_____
_____
_____
_____
_____
_____
_____
_____
_____
_____
_____
_____
_____
_____

GRAMMAR

Use the verbs in parentheses to complete the email. Use mixed conditionals.

Dear Elena,

Well, I'm halfway through my tour of Peru. I'd like to say that everything is going well, but unfortunately, that isn't the case. I think if I (1) ___**had prepared**___ (prepare) a little more thoroughly, I (2) _____ (enjoy) myself a lot more right now. I guess if I (3) _____ (take) more time to research where I was going to stay, I (4) _____ (have) a better time in this beautiful country.

My biggest mistake is that I didn't bring the right clothes. I brought all my summer clothes, and it is absolutely freezing! If I (5) _____ (bring) the right clothes, I (6) _____ (feel) more comfortable right now. Instead, I've been staying indoors as much as possible and have a terrible cold. I went to a local pharmacy to get some cold medicine, but I had some trouble reading the labels. I think I bought the wrong medicine. If I (7) _____ (buy) the right medicine, I (8) _____ (not sneeze) all the time! If I (9) _____ (follow) your advice about the weather and accommodations, I (10)_____ (not have) so many problems right now!

Anyway, I'll remember next time.
I miss you!

Love,
Sophia
Attached: perutrip014.jpg

GRAMMAR

Match the clauses to make conditional sentences. Write the correct letter.

1. If I had packed more carefully, _____
2. If I hadn't chosen a discount airline, _____
3. If I had studied English more often, _____
4. If I had left for the airport earlier, _____
5. If I hadn't forgotten my novel, _____

a. I wouldn't be afraid to ask people for directions.
b. I wouldn't be reading a boring magazine right now.
c. I wouldn't be searching my bags for my passport.
d. I would have a free movie to look forward to on board.
e. I wouldn't be worried about missing my flight!

VOCABULARY

What characteristics do you think would be most important for these people?
Write sentences about each picture using the adjectives from the box.

culturally aware	nonconforming	open-minded	self-motivated
culturally sensitive	nonjudgmental	self-assured	self-reliant

mountain climber

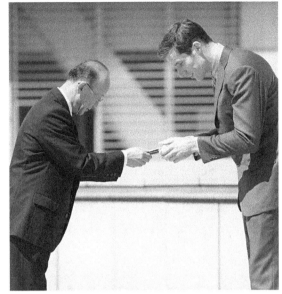
businessperson abroad

1. The mountain climber has to be _____*self-reliant*_____ because *she could be left*
   on her own in an emergency.

2. If the mountain climber weren't _____, she _____

3. The businessperson abroad should be _____

4. If the businessperson abroad weren't _____

GRAMMAR

Complete the sentences so they are true for you.

1. If I had been open-minded about *studying abroad in college, I would have*
   much more international experience on my résumé.

2. If I had been more self-assured when _____,
   I _____

3. If I had been more culturally aware when I was younger, I _____
   _____

4. If I hadn't been open-minded about _____,
   I _____

A Read the article quickly. Choose the tips that are mentioned.

☐ call your friends at home   ☐ spend a lot of time alone

☐ take a course in anthropology   ☐ prepare for culture shock

☐ take a class for people going abroad   ☐ visit a doctor regularly

BEATING CULTURE SHOCK

You have a chance to live and work overseas, to get to know another culture from the inside. It's a wonderful opportunity, but don't be surprised if you experience at least some culture shock. "When you're put into a new culture, even simple things will throw you. You become like a child again, unable to handle everyday life without help," says L. Robert Kohls, an expert on culture shock.

Taking an intercultural studies or anthropology course at a university or attending one of the many classes offered for people going abroad is an important way to reduce the stress of culture shock, says Elsie Purnell, the founder of a counseling agency. She advises people going overseas to expect culture shock and to try to be prepared for it.

Someone living in a new culture typically goes through four stages of adjustment. Initial euphoria, or the honeymoon stage, is characterized by high expectations, a focus on similarities in the new culture, and a tendency to attach positive values to any differences that are noticed.

Culture shock, the second stage, begins very suddenly. The symptoms of culture shock include homesickness, feelings of anxiety, depression, fatigue, and inadequacy. Some people going through culture shock try to withdraw from the new culture, spending most of their free time reading about home, sleeping 12 hours a night, and associating only with others from their own country. Others eat too much, feel irritable, and display hostility or even aggression.

A period of gradual adjustment is the third stage. Once you realize you're adjusting, life gets more hopeful. "You've been watching what's been going on, interpreting things, and you're starting to recognize the patterns and learn the underlying values of the culture," says Kohls. It feels more natural, and you feel more self-assured.

The fourth stage, full adjustment, can take several years, and not everyone achieves it. According to Kohls, a lot depends on people's personalities – how rigid or how easygoing they are – and how seriously they try to understand the new culture.

B Read the article again. At what stage would someone make the following statements?

	Stage 1	Stage 2	Stage 3	Stage 4
1. "I just want to sleep all the time."	☐	☑	☐	☐
2. "The customs here are different, but they are so wonderful and sophisticated!"	☐	☐	☐	☐
3. "I've lived here for so many years that it feels like home."	☐	☐	☐	☐
4. "Everyone has been so helpful and friendly since I've arrived. The people here are so polite!"	☐	☐	☐	☐
5. "I'm starting to understand the culture and feel more self-assured here."	☐	☐	☐	☐
6. "I only spend time with people from my own country."	☐	☐	☐	☐